U.S. Fish & Wildlife Service

I0439159

2006 National Survey of Fishing, Hunting, and Wildlife-Associated Recreation

Louisiana

FHW/06-LA
Issued March 2008

2006 National Survey of Fishing, Hunting, and Wildlife-Associated Recreation

Louisiana

U.S. Department of the Interior
Dirk Kempthorne,
Secretary

U.S. Fish and Wildlife Service
H. Dale Hall,
Director

U.S. Department of Commerce
Carlos M. Gutierrez,
Secretary

Economics and Statistics Administration
Cynthia A. Glassman,
Under Secretary for Economic Affairs

U.S. CENSUS BUREAU
Steve H. Murdock,
Director

**Economics and Statistics
Administration**

Cynthia A. Glassman,
Under Secretary for Economic Affairs

**U.S. CENSUS BUREAU
Steve H. Murdock,**
Director

**U.S. Department of the Interior
Dirk Kempthorne,**
Secretary

**U.S. Fish and Wildlife Service
H. Dale Hall,**
Director

**Wildlife and Sport Fish Restoration
Rowan Gould,**
Assistant Director

The U.S. Department of the Interior protects and manages the Nation's natural resources and cultural heritage; provides scientific and other information about those resources; and honors its trust responsibilities or special commitments to American Indians, Alaska Natives, and affiliated Island Communities.

The mission of the Department's U.S. Fish and Wildlife Service is working with others to conserve, protect, and enhance fish, wildlife, and their habitats for the continuing benefit of the American people. The Service is responsible for national programs of vital importance to our natural resources, including administration of the Wildlife and Sport Fish Restoration Programs. These two programs provide financial assistance to the States for projects to enhance and protect fish and wildlife resources and to assure their availability to the public for recreational purposes. Multistate grants from these programs fund the National Survey of Fishing, Hunting, and Wildlife-Associated Recreation.

Suggested Citation

U.S. Department of the Interior, Fish and Wildlife Service, and U.S. Department of Commerce, U.S. Census Bureau. 2006 National Survey of Fishing, Hunting, and Wildlife-Associated Recreation.

Contents

List of Tables. iv

Foreword vi

Survey Background and Method. vii

Highlights

Introduction. 2

Summary. 4

Wildlife-Associated Recreation 6

Sportspersons 7

Anglers 8

Hunters 10

Wildlife Watchers 12

1996–2006 Comparisons 14

Tables

Guide to Statistical Tables. 16

Fishing and Hunting Tables 17

Wildlife-Watching Tables 34

National Tables 43

Appendixes

A. Definitions. 48

B. 2005 Participation of 6- to 15-Year-Olds: Data From Screening Interviews 52

C. Significant Methodological Changes From Previous Surveys and Regional Trends 58

D. Sample Design and Statistical Accuracy. 66

List of Tables

Fishing and Hunting

1. Fishing and Hunting in Louisiana by Resident and Nonresident Sportspersons: 2006 17
2. Anglers and Hunters, Days of Participation, and Trips in Louisiana by Type of Fishing
   and Hunting: 2006. 17
3. Anglers and Hunters, Trips, and Days of Participation: 2006. 18
4. Louisiana Resident Anglers and Hunters by Place Fished or Hunted: 2006. 18
5. Louisiana Resident Anglers and Hunters, Days of Participation, and Trips in the
   United States by Type of Fishing and Hunting: 2006 19
6. Freshwater Anglers, Trips, Days of Fishing, and Type of Water Fished: 2006. 19
7. Freshwater Anglers and Days of Fishing in Louisiana by Type of Fish: 2006 20
8. Great Lakes Anglers, Trips, and Days of Fishing in Louisiana: 2006. 21
9. Great Lakes Anglers and Days of Fishing in Louisiana by Type of Fish: 2006 21
10. Saltwater Anglers, Trips, and Days of Fishing in Louisiana: 2006. 22
11. Saltwater Anglers and Days of Fishing in Louisiana by Type of Fish: 2006 22
12. Hunters, Trips, and Days of Hunting in Louisiana by Type of Hunting: 2006 23
13. Hunters and Days of Hunting in Louisiana by Type of Game: 2006 24
14. Hunters and Days of Hunting in Louisiana by Type of Land: 2006 24
15. Selected Characteristics of Louisiana Resident Anglers and Hunters: 2006. 25
16. Summary of Expenditures in Louisiana by State Residents and Nonresidents Combined for
    Fishing and Hunting: 2006 26
17. Summary of Fishing Trip and Equipment Expenditures in Louisiana by State Residents and
    Nonresidents Combined by Type of Fishing: 2006. 27
18. Summary of Hunting Trip and Equipment Expenditures in Louisiana by State Residents and
    Nonresidents Combined by Type of Hunting: 2006 28
19. Expenditures in Louisiana by State Residents and Nonresidents Combined for Fishing: 2006. 29
20. Expenditures in Louisiana by State Residents and Nonresidents Combined for Hunting: 2006 30
21. Trip and Equipment Expenditures in Louisiana for Fishing and Hunting by Louisiana Residents
    and Nonresidents: 2006. 31
22. Summary of Louisiana Residents' Fishing and Hunting Expenditures Both Inside and Outside
    Louisiana: 2006. 32
23. In-State and Out-of-State Expenditures by Louisiana Residents for Fishing and Hunting: 2006 33

Wildlife Watching

24. Wildlife Watching in Louisiana by State Residents and Nonresidents Combined: 2006 34
25. Participants, Trips, and Days of Participation in Away-From-Home Wildlife Watching in
    Louisiana: 2006. 34
26. Away-From-Home Wildlife-Watching Participants by Wildlife Observed, Photographed, or
    Fed in Louisiana: 2006 35

27. Participation in Wildlife-Watching Activities Around the Home in Louisiana: 2006 36

28. Louisiana Residents Participating in Wildlife Watching in the United States: 2006 36

29. Wild Bird Observers and Days of Observation in Louisiana by State Residents and
     Nonresidents: 2006 37

30. Selected Characteristics of Louisiana Residents Participating in Wildlife Watching: 2006 38

31. Expenditures in Louisiana by State Residents and Nonresidents Combined for Wildlife
     Watching: 2006 39

32. Trip and Equipment Expenditures in Louisiana for Wildlife Watching by Louisiana Residents
     and Nonresidents: 2006 40

33. Wildlife-Watching Expenditures Both Inside and Outside Louisiana by Louisiana
     Residents: 2006 41

34. In-State and Out-of-State Expenditures by Louisiana Residents for Wildlife Watching: 2006 42

35. Participation of Louisiana Resident Wildlife-Watching Participants in Fishing and
     Hunting: 2006 42

36. Participation of Louisiana Resident Sportspersons in Wildlife-Watching Activities: 2006 42

National Tables

37. Participation in Wildlife-Associated Recreation by State Residents Both Inside and Outside
     Their Resident State: 2006 43

38. Anglers and Hunters by Sportsperson's State of Residence: 2006 44

39. Participation in Wildlife-Associated Recreation in Each State by Both Residents and
     Nonresidents of the State: 2006 45

40. Anglers and Hunters by State Where Fishing or Hunting Took Place: 2006 46

Foreword

I find duck hunting with friends in a bottomland hardwood swamp or fishing with my kids on an Oregon river bolsters my spirit and reminds me why I care about conservation and our wildlife heritage.

But wildlife-associated and vital recreation—activities such as hunting, fishing, and birding—also provide significant financial support for wildlife conservation in our Nation's economy. According to information from the newest National Survey of Fishing, Hunting, and Wildlife-Associated Recreation, 87.5 million Americans spent more than $122 billion in 2006 on wildlife-related recreation. And this spending supports hundreds of thousands of jobs in industries and businesses.

The Survey is conducted every five years at the request of State fish and wildlife agencies to measure the importance of wildlife-based recreation to the American people. The 2006 Survey represents the 11th in a series that began in 1955. Developed in collaboration with the States, the Association of Fish and Wildlife Agencies, and national conservation organizations, the Survey has become one of the most important sources of information on fish and wildlife-related recreation in the United States.

In the 75-year history of the Sport Fish and Wildlife Restoration Programs, excise taxes on firearms, ammunition, archery, and angling equipment have generated a cumulative total of more than $10 billion for wildlife conservation efforts by State and Territorial wildlife agencies for fish and wildlife management.

My thanks go to the men and women who took time to participate in the survey, as well as to the State fish and wildlife agencies for their financial support through the Multistate Conservation Grant Programs. Without that support, the 2006 Survey would never have been possible.

I am comforted to know that my children and all Americans will have the opportunity to appreciate our Nation's rich wildlife tradition. Along with a record number of Americans, we continue to enjoy wildlife. We are laying the foundation for conservation's future.

H. Dale Hall
Director, U.S. Fish and Wildlife Service

Survey Background and Method

The National Survey of Fishing, Hunting, and Wildlife-Associated Recreation (Survey) has been conducted since 1955 and is one of the oldest and most comprehensive continuing recreation surveys. The Survey collects information on the number of anglers, hunters, and wildlife watchers; how often they participate; and how much they spend on their activities in the United States.

Preparations for the 2006 Survey began in 2004 when the Association of Fish and Wildlife Agencies (AFWA) recommended that the Fish and Wildlife Service conduct the 11th Survey of wildlife-related recreation. Funding came from the Multistate Conservation Grant Programs, authorized by Sport Fish and Wildlife Restoration Acts, as amended.

We consulted with State and Federal agencies and nongovernmental organizations such as the Wildlife Management Institute and American Sportfishing Association to determine survey content. Other sportspersons' organizations and conservation groups, industry representatives, and researchers also provided valuable advice.

Four regional technical committees were set up under the auspices of the AFWA to ensure that State fish and wildlife agencies had an opportunity to participate in all phases of survey planning and design. The committees were made up of agency representatives.

Data collection for the Survey was carried out by the U.S. Census Bureau in two phases. The first phase was the screen which began in April 2006. During this phase, the Census Bureau interviewed a sample of 85,000 households nationwide to determine who in the household had fished, hunted, or wildlife watched in 2005, and who had engaged or planned to engage in those activities in 2006. In most cases, one adult household member provided information for all members. The screen primarily covered 2005 activities while the next, more in-depth phase covered 2006 activities. For more information on 2005 data, refer to Appendix B.

The second phase of data collection consisted of three detailed interview waves. The first began in April 2006 concurrent with the screen, the second in September 2006, and the last in January 2007. Interviews were conducted with samples of likely anglers, hunters, and wildlife watchers who were identified in the initial screening phase. Interviews were conducted primarily by phone, with in-person interviews for respondents who could not be reached by phone. Respondents in the second survey phase were limited to those who were at least 16 years old. Each respondent provided information pertaining only to his or her activities and expenditures. Sample sizes were designed to provide statistically reliable results at the state level. Information on sampling procedures, sample sizes, and response rates is found in Appendix D.

Comparability With Previous Surveys

The 2006 Survey questions and methodology were similar to those used in the 2001, 1996, and 1991 Surveys. Therefore, the estimates are comparable.

The methodology of these Surveys did differ importantly from the 1985 and 1980 Surveys, so these estimates are not directly comparable to those of earlier surveys. Changes in methodology included reducing the recall period over which respondents had to report their activities and expenditures. Previous Surveys used a 12-month recall period, which resulted in greater reporting bias. Research found that the amount of activity and expenditures reported in 12-month recall surveys was overestimated in comparison with that reported using shorter recall periods.

Highlights

Introduction

The National Survey of Fishing, Hunting, and Wildlife-Associated Recreation reports results from interviews with U.S. residents about their fishing, hunting, and wildlife watching. This report focuses on 2006 participation and expenditures of persons 16 years of age and older.

The Survey is a snapshot of one year. The information it collected tells us how many people participated and how much they spent on their activities in the State in 2006. It does not tell us how many anglers, hunters, and wildlife watchers there were because many do not participate every year. For example, based on information collected by the Survey's household screen and detailed phase, we can estimate that about 33 percent more anglers and hunters participated nationally in at least 1 of the 4 years prior to the survey year 2006.

In addition to 2006 estimates, we also provide trend information in the Highlights section and Appendix C of the report. The 2006 numbers reported can be compared with those in the 1991, 1996, and 2001 Survey reports because they used similar methodologies. The 2006 estimates should not be directly compared with results from Surveys conducted earlier than 1991 because of changes in methodology to improve accuracy.

The report also provides information on participation in wildlife recreation in 2005, particularly of persons 6 to 15 years of age. The 2005 information is provided in Appendix B. Information about the Survey's scope and coverage is in Appendix D. The remainder of this section defines important terms used in the Survey.

This report does not provide information about the State's wildlife resources. That, and additional information on wildlife-related recreation, may be obtained from State fish and wildlife agencies. The Association of Fish and Wildlife Agencies can provide the addresses and telephone numbers of those agencies. The Association's Web site is <www.fishwildlife.org>.

Wildlife-Associated Recreation

Wildlife-associated recreation is fishing, hunting, and wildlife-watching activities. These categories are not mutually exclusive because many individuals participated in more than one activity. Wildlife-associated recreation is reported in two major categories: (1) fishing and hunting and (2) wildlife watching, which includes observing, photographing, and feeding fish or wildlife.

Fishing and Hunting

This Survey reports information about residents of the United States who fished or hunted in 2006, regardless of whether they were licensed. The fishing and hunting sections report information for three groups: (1) sportspersons, (2) anglers, and (3) hunters.

Sportspersons

Sportspersons are those who fished or hunted. Individuals who fished or hunted commercially in 2006 are reported as sportspersons only if they also fished or hunted for recreation. The sportspersons group is composed of three subgroups, as shown in the diagram on this page: (1) those that fished and hunted, (2) those that only fished, and (3) those that only hunted.

The total number of sportspersons is equal to the sum of people who only fished, only hunted, and both hunted and fished. It is not the sum of all anglers and all hunters because those people who both fished and hunted are included in both the angler and hunter population and would be incorrectly counted twice.

Sportspersons

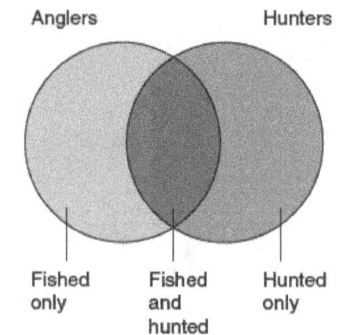

Anglers   Hunters

Fished only   Fished and hunted   Hunted only

Anglers

Anglers are sportspersons who only fished plus those who fished and hunted. Anglers include not only licensed hook and line anglers, but also those who have no license and those who use special methods such as fishing with spears.

Three types of fishing are reported: (1) freshwater, excluding the Great Lakes, (2) Great Lakes, and (3) saltwater. Since many anglers participated in more than one type of fishing, the total number of anglers is less than the sum of the three types of fishing.

Hunters

Hunters are sportspersons who only hunted plus those who hunted and fished. Hunters include not only licensed hunters using rifles and shotguns but also those who had no license and those who hunted with a bow and arrow, primitive firearm, or pistol or handgun.

Four types of hunting are reported: (1) big game, (2) small game, (3) migratory bird, and (4) other animals. Since many hunters participated in more than one type of hunting, the sum of hunters for big game, small game, migratory bird, and other animals exceeds the total number of hunters.

Wildlife Watchers

Since 1980, the National Survey has included information on wildlife-watching activities in addition to fishing and hunting. The 1991, 1996, 2001, and 2006 Surveys, unlike the 1980 and 1985 Surveys, collected data only for activities where the *primary* purpose was wildlife watching. The 1980 and 1985 Surveys included estimates of unplanned wildlife watching around the home and while on trips taken for another purpose.

The 2006 Survey uses a strict definition of wildlife watching. Participants must either take a "special interest" in wildlife around their homes or take a trip for the "primary purpose" of wildlife watching. Secondary wildlife watching, such as incidentally observing wildlife while pleasure driving, is not included.

Two types of wildlife watching are reported: (1) away-from-home (formerly nonresidential) activities and (2) around-the-home (formerly residential) activities. Because some people participated in more than one type of wildlife watching, the sum of participants in each type will be greater than the total number of wildlife watchers. The two types of wildlife-watching activity are explained next.

Away-From-Home Wildlife Watching

This group includes persons who took trips or outings of at least 1 mile from home for the primary purpose of observing, feeding, or photographing fish and wildlife. Trips to fish, hunt, or scout and trips to zoos, circuses, aquariums, and museums are not considered wildlife-watching activities.

Around-the-Home Wildlife Watching

This group includes those who participated within 1 mile of home and involves one or more of the following: (1) closely observing or trying to identify birds or other wildlife; (2) photographing wildlife; (3) feeding birds or other wildlife; (4) maintaining natural areas of at least 1/4 acre where benefit to wildlife is the primary concern; (5) maintaining plantings (shrubs, agricultural crops, etc.) where benefit to wildlife is the primary concern; or (6) visiting public parks within 1 mile of home for the primary purpose of observing, feeding, or photographing wildlife.

2006 Louisiana Summary

Activities in Louisiana by Residents and Nonresidents

Fishing

Anglers............................... **702,000**
Days of fishing 11,204,000
Average days per angler 16
Total expenditures................$1,006,136,000
   Trip-related $337,363,000
   Equipment and other........... $668,773,000
Average per angler $1,416
Average trip expenditure per day $30

Hunting

Hunters............................. **270,000**
Days of hunting...................... 5,979,000
Average days per hunter 22
Total expenditures............... $525,505,000
   Trip-related $205,355,000
   Equipment and other........... $320,150,000
Average per hunter $1,904
Average trip expenditure per day $34

Wildlife Watching

Total wildlife-watching participants **738,000**
   Away-from-home participants......... 225,000
   Around-the-home participants......... 671,000
Days of participation away from home..... 3,199,000
Average days of participation
  away from home 14
Total expenditures................. $312,430,000
   Trip-related $61,822,000
   Equipment and other........... $250,608,000
Average per participant................... $422
Average trip expenditure per day $19

Activities in Louisiana by Nonresidents

Fishing

Anglers............................... **112,000**
Days of fishing 640,000
Average days per angler 6
Total expenditures.................. $249,337,000
   Trip-related $78,434,000
   Equipment and other............ $170,903,000
Average per angler $2,233
Average trip expenditure per day $123

Hunting

Hunters............................... **...**
Days of hunting ....
Average days per hunter ....
Total expenditures.................. [1]$37,125,000
   Trip-related ....
   Equipment and other.................. ...
Average per hunter ....
Average trip expenditure per day ....

Wildlife Watching

Total wildlife-watching participants .... **...**
   Away-from-home participants............ ...
   Around-the-home participants............ ...
Days of participation away from home........ ...
Average days of participation
  away from home ....
Total expenditures........................ ...
   Trip-related ....
   Equipment and other.................. ...
Average per participant.................... ...
Average trip expenditure per day ....

[1] Expenditures are reportable because nonresident anglers bought
hunting-related items in Louisiana but did not hunt there.

... Sample size too small to report data reliably.

Activities in Louisiana by Residents

Fishing

Anglers............................... **590,000**
Days of fishing 10,564,000
Average days per angler 18
Total expenditures.................. $756,799,000
   Trip-related $258,929,000
   Equipment and other............. $497,870,000
Average per angler $1,283
Average trip expenditure per day $25

Hunting

Hunters............................. **241,000**
Days of hunting...................... 5,847,000
Average days per hunter 24
Total expenditures.................. $488,380,000
   Trip-related $193,365,000
   Equipment and other............. $295,015,000
Average per hunter $2,027
Average trip expenditure per day $33

Wildlife Watching

Total wildlife-watching participants **706,000**
   Away-from-home participants.......... 193,000
   Around-the-home participants......... 671,000
Days of participation away from home..... 3,076,000
Average days of participation
  away from home 16
Total expenditures.................. $276,145,000
   Trip-related $26,859,000
   Equipment and other............. $249,286,000
Average per participant..................... $391
Average trip expenditure per day $9

Activities by Louisiana Residents Both Inside and Outside Louisiana

Fishing

Anglers............................... **598,000**
Days of fishing 11,075,000
Average days per angler 19
Total expenditures.................. $807,063,000
   Trip-related $289,431,000
   Equipment and other............. $517,632,000
Average per angler $1,350
Average trip expenditure per day $26

Hunting

Hunters............................. **275,000**
Days of hunting...................... 7,155,000
Average days per hunter 26
Total expenditures.................. $618,264,000
   Trip-related $273,863,000
   Equipment and other............. $344,401,000
Average per hunter $2,244
Average trip expenditure per day $38

Wildlife Watching

Total wildlife-watching participants **712,000**
   Away-from-home participants.......... 234,000
   Around-the-home participants......... 671,000
Days of participation away from home..... 3,905,000
Average days of participation
  away from home 17
Total expenditures.................. $420,881,000
   Trip-related $118,317,000
   Equipment and other............. $302,564,000
Average per participant..................... $591
Average trip expenditure per day $30

Wildlife-Associated Recreation

Participation in Louisiana

The 2006 Survey found that 1.2 million Louisiana residents and nonresidents 16 years old and older fished, hunted, or wildlife watched in Louisiana. Of the total number of participants, 702 thousand fished, 270 thousand hunted, and 738 thousand participated in wildlife-watching activities, which include observing, feeding, and photographing wildlife. The sum of anglers, hunters, and wildlife watchers exceeds the total number of participants in wildlife-related recreation because many individuals engaged in more than one wildlife-related activity.

Participation by 6-to-15-Year-Old Louisiana Residents

The focus of the National Survey is on the activity of participants 16 years old and older. However, the activity of 6- to 15-year-olds can be calculated using the screening data covering the year 2005. It is assumed for estimation purposes that the relative activity levels of 6-to-15-year-old participants

and participants 16 years old and older remained the same in 2005 and 2006. Based on this assumption, in addition to the 598 thousand resident anglers 16 years old and older, there were 133 thousand resident anglers 6 to 15 years old. Also, in addition to the 275 thousand residents 16 years old and older who hunted, there were 43 thousand 6-to-15-year-old residents who hunted. Finally, there were 712 thousand Louisiana residents 16 years old and older and 127 thousand 6- to 15-year-olds who wildlife watched. Further information on 6- to 15-year-olds is provided in Appendix B.

Expenditures in Louisiana

In 2006, state residents and nonresidents spent $2.0 billion on wildlife recreation in Louisiana. Of that total, trip-related expenditures were $605 million and equipment purchases totaled $990 million. The remaining $429 million was spent on licenses, contributions, land ownership and leasing, and other items.

Percent of Total Participants by Activity
(Total: 1.2 million participants)

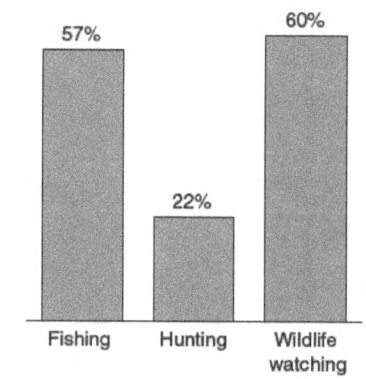

Fishing	Hunting	Wildlife watching
57%	22%	60%

Participants in Wildlife-Associated Recreation in Louisiana: 2006
(U.S. residents 16 years old and older)

Total	1.2 million
Sportspersons	
Total	769 thousand
Anglers	702 thousand
Hunters	270 thousand
Wildlife Watchers	
Total	738 thousand
Away from home	225 thousand
Around the home	671 thousand

Note: Detail does not add to total because of multiple responses.

Source: Tables 3, 24, and 39.

Wildlife-Associated Recreation Expenditures in Louisiana
(Total: $2.0 billion)

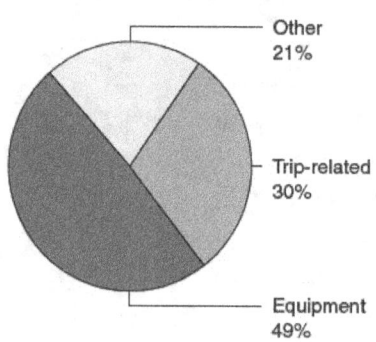

Other 21%

Trip-related 30%

Equipment 49%

Sportspersons

In 2006, 769 thousand state resident and nonresident sportspersons 16 years old and older fished or hunted in Louisiana. This group comprised 702 thousand anglers (91 percent of all sportspersons) and 270 thousand hunters (35 percent of all sportspersons). Among the 769 thousand sportspersons who fished or hunted in the state, 499 thousand (65 percent) fished but did not hunt in Louisiana. Another 68 thousand (9 percent) hunted but did not fish there. The remaining 203 thousand (26 percent) fished and hunted in Louisiana in 2006.

Sportspersons' Participation in Louisiana
(State residents and nonresidents 16 years old and older)

Sportspersons (fished or hunted)	**769 thousand**
Anglers	**702 thousand**
Fished only	499 thousand
Fished and hunted	203 thousand
Hunters	**270 thousand**
Hunted only	68 thousand
Hunted and fished	203 thousand

Note: Detail does not add to total because of multiple responses.

Source: Table 1.

Anglers

Participants and Days of Fishing

In 2006, 702 thousand state residents and nonresidents 16 years old and older fished in Louisiana. Of this total, 590 thousand anglers (84 percent) were state residents and 112 thousand anglers (16 percent) were nonresidents. Anglers fished a total of 11.2 million days in Louisiana—an average of 16 days per angler. State residents fished 10.6 million days—94 percent of all fishing days in Louisiana.

Nonresidents fished 640 thousand days in Louisiana—6 percent of all fishing days in the state.

A large majority of Louisiana residents who fished anywhere in the United States did so in their resident state. There were 598 thousand Louisiana residents 16 years old and older who fished in the United States in 2006 for a total of 11.1 million days. An estimated 99 percent of all Louisiana residents who fished did so in their home state.

Of all fishing days by Louisiana residents, 95 percent or 10.6 million were in their home state.

Some state residents fished in states other than Louisiana. In 2006, 64 thousand Louisiana residents fished in other states—11 percent of all residents fishing in any state. They fished 641 thousand days as nonresidents, representing 6 percent of all days fished by Louisiana residents. For further details about fishing in Louisiana, see Table 3.

Anglers in Louisiana
(State residents and nonresidents 16 years old and older)

Anglers	**702 thousand**
Resident	590 thousand
Nonresident	112 thousand
Days of fishing	**11.2 million**
Resident	10.6 million
Nonresident	640 thousand

Source: Table 3.

In State/Out of State
(State residents 16 years old and older)

Louisiana anglers	**598 thousand**
In Louisiana	590 thousand
In other states	64 thousand
Days of fishing	**11.1 million**
In Louisiana	10.6 million
In other states	641 thousand

Note: Detail does not add to total because of multiple responses.

Source: Table 3.

Fishing Expenditures in Louisiana

All fishing-related expenditures in Louisiana totaled $1.0 billion in 2006. Trip-related expenditures, which include food and lodging, transportation, and other trip expenses, totaled $337 million—34 percent of all fishing expenditures. Expenditures for food and lodging were $97 million and transportation expenditures were $87 million. Other trip expenses, such as equipment rental, bait, and cooking fuel, totaled $153 million. Each angler spent an average of $481 on trip-related costs during 2006.

Anglers spent $425 million on equipment in Louisiana in 2006, 42 percent of all fishing expenditures. Fishing equipment (rods, reels, line, etc.) spending totaled $122 million—29 percent of the equipment total. Auxiliary equipment expenditures (tents, special fishing clothes, etc.) and special equipment expenditures (boats, vans, etc.) amounted to $302 million—71 percent of the equipment total. Special and auxiliary equipment are items that were purchased for fishing but could be used in activities other than fishing.

The purchase of other items, such as magazines, membership dues, licenses, permits, stamps, and land leasing and ownership, amounted to $244 million—24 percent of all fishing expenditures. For more details about fishing expenditures in Louisiana, see Tables 19 and 21 through 23.

Fishing Expenditures in Louisiana
(State residents and nonresidents 16 years old and older)

Total	$1.0 billion
Trip-related	$337 million
Equipment	$425 million
Fishing	$122 million
Auxiliary and special	$302 million
Other	$244 million

Source: Table 19.

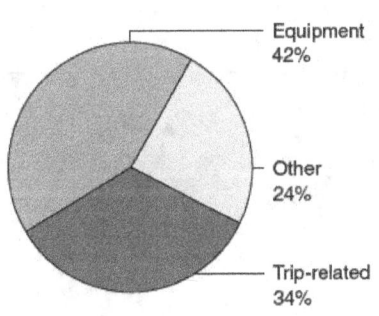

Fishing Expenditures in Louisiana
(Total: $1.0 billion)

Equipment 42%
Other 24%
Trip-related 34%

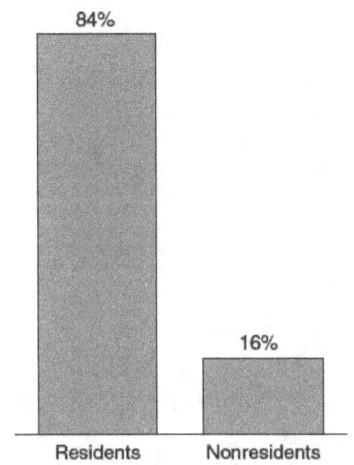

Percent of Anglers by Residence
(Total: 702 thousand participants)

84% Residents
16% Nonresidents

Hunters

Participants and Days of Hunting

In 2006, there were 270 thousand residents and nonresidents 16 years old and older who hunted in Louisiana. Resident hunters numbered 241 thousand, accounting for 89 percent of the hunters in Louisiana. Residents and nonresidents hunted 6.0 million days in 2006, an average of 22 days per hunter. Residents hunted 5.8 million days in Louisiana or 98 percent of all hunting days.

There were 275 thousand Louisiana residents 16 years old and older who hunted in the United States in 2006 for a total of 7.2 million days. An estimated 87 percent of all Louisiana residents who hunted did so in their home state. Of all hunting days by Louisiana residents, 82 percent or 5.8 million were spent pursuing game in their home state.

Some state residents hunted in states other than Louisiana. Altogether, 75 thousand or 27 percent of all Louisiana hunters hunted in other states. Their 1.4 million days of hunting in other states represented 20 percent of all days Louisiana residents spent hunting in 2006. For more information on hunting activities by Louisiana residents, see Table 3.

Hunters in Louisiana
(State residents and nonresidents 16 years old and older)

Hunters	**270 thousand**
Resident	241 thousand
Nonresident	...
Days of hunting	**6.0 million**
Resident	5.8 million
Nonresident	...

... Sample size too small to report data reliably.

Source: Table 3.

In State/Out of State
(State residents 16 years old and older)

Louisiana hunters	**275 thousand**
In Louisiana	241 thousand
In other states	75 thousand
Days of hunting	**7.2 million**
In Louisiana	5.8 million
In other states	1.4 million

Note: Detail does not add to total because of multiple responses.

Source: Table 3.

Hunting Expenditures in Louisiana

All hunting-related expenditures in Louisiana totaled $526 million in 2006. Trip-related expenses, such as food and lodging, transportation, and other trip expenses, totaled $205 million—39 percent of total expenditures. Expenditures for food and lodging were $83 million and transportation expenditures were $74 million. Other trip expenses, such as equipment rental, totaled $48 million for the year. The average trip-related expenditure per hunter was $759.

Hunters spent $206 million on equipment—39 percent of all hunting expenditures. Hunting equipment (guns, ammunition, etc.) totaled $115 million and made up 56 percent of all equipment costs. Hunters spent $91 million on auxiliary equipment (tents, special hunting clothes, etc.) and special equipment (boats, vans, etc.), accounting for 44 percent of total equipment expenditures for hunting. Special and auxiliary equipment are items that were purchased for hunting but could be used in activities other than hunting.

The purchase of other items, such as magazines, membership dues, licenses, permits, and land leasing and ownership, cost hunters $114 million—22 percent of all hunting expenditures. For more details on hunting expenditures in Louisiana, see Tables 20 through 23.

Hunting Expenditures in Louisiana
(State residents and nonresidents 16 years old and older)

Total	$526 million
Trip-related	$205 million
Equipment	$206 million
Hunting	$115 million
Auxiliary and special	$91 million
Other	$114 million

Source: Table 20.

Hunting Expenditures in Louisiana
(Total: $526 million)

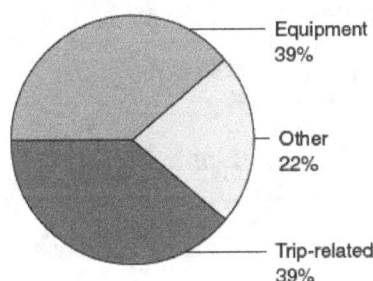

Equipment 39%

Other 22%

Trip-related 39%

Wildlife Watchers

Participants and Days of Activity

In 2006, 738 thousand U.S. residents 16 years old and older fed, observed, or photographed wildlife in Louisiana. Most of them, 91 percent (671 thousand), enjoyed their activities close to home and are called "around-the-home" participants. Those persons who enjoyed wildlife at least 1 mile from home are called "away-from-home" participants. People participating in away-from-home activities in Louisiana in 2006 numbered 225 thousand—30 percent of all wildlife watchers in Louisiana. Of the 225 thousand, 193 thousand were state residents.

Louisiana residents 16 years old and older who enjoyed away-from-home wildlife watching within their state totaled 193 thousand. Of this group, 168 thousand participants observed wildlife and 106 thousand fed wildlife. Since some individuals engaged in more than one of the away-from-home activities during the year, the sum of wildlife observers and feeders exceeds the total number of away-from-home participants.

Louisiana residents spent 3.1 million days engaged in away-from-home wildlife-watching activities in their state. They spent 1.5 million days observing wildlife, and additional days were spent feeding and photographing wildlife. For further details about away-from-home activities, see Table 25.

Louisiana residents also took an active interest in wildlife around their homes. In 2006, 671 thousand state residents enjoyed observing, feeding, and photographing wildlife within 1 mile of their homes. Among this around-the-home group, 598 thousand fed, 491 thousand observed, and 125 thousand photographed wildlife around their homes. Another 162 thousand participants maintained natural areas of 1/4 acre or more for wildlife, and 155 thousand participants maintained plantings for the benefit of wildlife. Summing the number of participants in these around-the-home activities results in an estimate that exceeds the total number of around-the-home participants because many people participated in more than

---

Wildlife-Watching Participants in Louisiana
(State residents and nonresidents 16 years old and older)

Total	**738 thousand**
Around the home.	671 thousand
Away from home	225 thousand

Note: Detail does not add to total because of multiple responses.

Source: Table 24.

Away-From-Home Wildlife-Watching Participation in Louisiana
(State residents and nonresidents 16 years old and older)

Participants, total	**225 thousand**
Observe wildlife	200 thousand
Feed wildlife	116 thousand
Photograph wildlife.	82 thousand
Days, total	**3.2 million**
Observe wildlife	1.6 million
Feed wildlife	1.1 million
Photograph wildlife.	814 thousand

Note: Detail does not add to total because of multiple responses.

Source: Table 25.

Around-the-Home Wildlife-Watching Participation in Louisiana
(State residents 16 years old and older)

Total	**671 thousand**
Feed wildlife	598 thousand
Observe wildlife	491 thousand
Photograph wildlife.	125 thousand
Maintain natural areas.	162 thousand
Maintain plantings.	155 thousand
Visit public areas.	...

... Sample size too small to report data reliably.

Note: Detail does not add to total because of multiple responses.

Source: Table 27.

one type of around-the-home activity. In addition, 29 percent of resident around-the-home wildlife watchers also enjoyed wildlife away from home. For further details about Louisiana residents participating in around-the-home wildlife-watching activities, see Table 27.

Wild Bird Observers

Bird watching attracted many wildlife enthusiasts in Louisiana. In 2006, 552 thousand people observed birds around the home and on trips in the state. Of these, 85 percent (467 thousand) observed wild birds around the home while 36 percent (197 thousand) took trips away from home to watch birds.

Wildlife-Watching Expenditures in Louisiana

Wildlife watchers spent $312 million on wildlife-watching activities in Louisiana in 2006. Twenty percent, $62 million, was for trip-related related expenses, including food and lodging ($42 million) and transportation ($19 million). The average of the trip-related expenditures for away-from-home participants was $275 per person in 2006.

Wildlife-watching participants spent $188 million on equipment—60 percent of all their expenditures. Specifically, wildlife-watching equipment (binoculars, special clothing, etc.) expenditures totaled $102 million, 54 percent of the equipment total.

Other items purchased by wildlife-watching participants, such as magazines, membership dues and contributions, land leasing and ownership, and plantings, totaled $62 million—20 percent of all wildlife-watching expenditures. For more details about wildlife-watching expenditures in Louisiana, see Table 31.

Wild Bird Observers in Louisiana
(State residents and nonresidents 16 years old and older)

Participants, total	**552 thousand**
Around the home.	467 thousand
Away from home.	197 thousand
Days, total	**68.3 million**
Around the home.	65.5 million
Away from home.	2.8 million

Note: Detail does not add to total because of multiple responses.

Source: Table 29.

Wildlife-Watching Expenditures in Louisiana
(State residents and nonresidents 16 years old and older)

Total	**$312 million**
Trip-related	$62 million
Equipment.	$188 million
Wildlife watching.	$102 million
Auxiliary and special	...
Other	$62 million

... Sample size too small to report data reliably.

Source: Table 31.

Around-the-Home and Away-From-Home Participation by Louisiana Residents
(Total: 671 thousand participants)

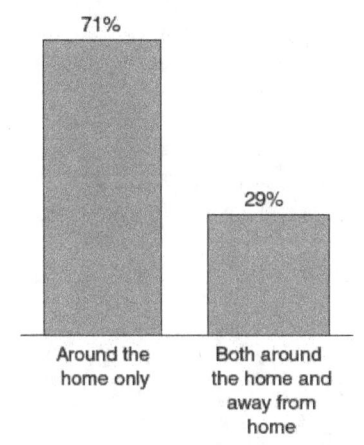

Wildlife-Watching Expenditures in Louisiana
(Total: $312 million)

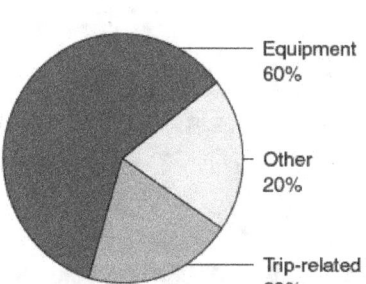

Equipment 60%

Other 20%

Trip-related 20%

1996–2006 Comparisons

Comparing the estimates from the 1996, 2001, and 2006 Surveys gives a perspective on the state of wildlife-related recreation in the late 1990s and early-to-mid 2000s in Louisiana. Only the most general recreation comparisons are presented here.

The best way to compare estimates from surveys is not to compare the estimates themselves but to compare the confidence intervals around the estimates. A 90-percent confidence interval around an estimate gives the range of estimates that 90 percent of all possible representative samples would supply. If the 90-percent confidence intervals of two surveys' estimates overlap, it is not possible to say the two estimates are statistically different.

The state resident estimates cover the participation and expenditure activity of Louisiana residents anywhere in the United States. The in-state estimates cover the participation, day, and expenditure activity of U.S. residents in Louisiana.

The expenditure estimates were made comparable by adjusting the estimates for inflation—all estimates are in 2006 dollars.

Louisiana 1996 and 2006 Comparison
(Numbers in thousands)

	1996	2006	Percent change
Fishing			
Anglers in state	1,031	702	–32
Days in state	20,987	11,204	–47
In-state expenditures by U.S. anglers	$1,061,915	$1,006,136	*
State resident anglers	860	598	–30
Total expenditures by state residents	$1,155,357	$807,063	*
Hunting			
Hunters in state	352	270	*
Days in state	6,756	5,979	*
In-state expenditures by U.S. hunters	$743,409	$525,505	*
State resident hunters	366	275	–25
Total expenditures by state residents	$821,472	$618,264	*
Away-From-Home Wildlife Watching			
Participants in state	260	225	*
Days in state	2,713	3,199	*
State resident participants	306	234	*
Around-the-Home Wildlife Watching			
Total participants	835	671	–20
Observers	624	491	*
Feeders	756	598	–21
Wildlife-Watching Expenditures			
In-state expenditures by U.S. wildlife watchers	$255,938	$312,430	*
Total expenditures by state residents	$332,889	$420,881	*

* Not different from zero at the 10 percent level of significance.

Louisiana 2001 and 2006 Comparison
(Numbers in thousands)

	2001	2006	Percent change
Fishing			
Anglers in state	970	702	–28
Days in state	12,637	11,204	*
In-state expenditures by U.S. anglers	$801,845	$1,006,136	*
State resident anglers	763	598	–22
Total expenditures by state residents	$739,045	$807,063	*
Hunting			
Hunters in state	333	270	*
Days in state	6,442	5,979	*
In-state expenditures by U.S. hunters	$508,673	$525,505	*
State resident hunters	316	275	*
Total expenditures by state residents	$602,097	$618,264	*
Away-From-Home Wildlife Watching			
Participants in state	314	225	*
Days in state	2,432	3,199	*
State resident participants	250	234	*
Around-the-Home Wildlife Watching			
Total participants	806	671	*
Observers	505	491	*
Feeders	714	598	*
Wildlife-Watching Expenditures			
In-state expenditures by U.S. wildlife watchers	$191,999	$312,430	*
Total expenditures by state residents	$213,995	$420,881	*

* Not different from zero at the 10 percent level of significance.

Number of People Who Hunted and Fished in Louisiana: 1996–2006
(In thousands)

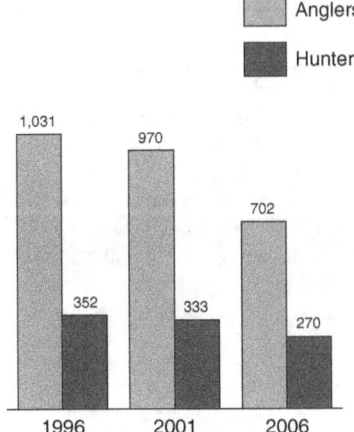

Number of People Who Wildlife Watched in Louisiana: 1996–2006
(In thousands)

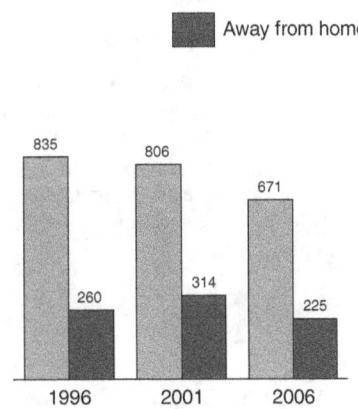

Total Expenditures by Participants in Louisiana
(In millions of 2006 dollars)

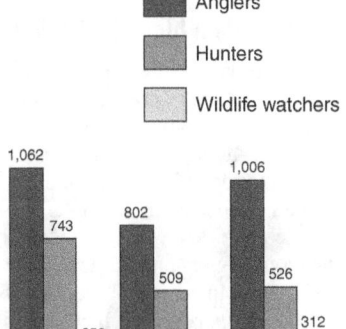

Guide to Statistical Tables

Purpose and Coverage of Tables

The statistical tables of this report were designed to meet a wide range of needs for those interested in wildlife-related recreation. Special terms used in these tables are defined in Appendix A.

The tables are based on responses to the 2006 Survey, which was designed to collect data about participation in wildlife-related recreation. To have taken part in the Survey, a respondent must have been a U.S. resident (a resident of one of the 50 states or the District of Columbia). No one residing outside the United States (including U.S. citizens) was eligible for interviewing. Therefore, reported state and national totals do not include participation by those who were not U.S. residents or who were U.S. citizens residing outside the United States.

Comparability With Previous Surveys

The numbers reported can be compared with those in the 1991, 1996, and 2001 Survey Reports. The methodology used in 2006 was similar to that used in those Surveys. These results should not be directly compared to results from Surveys earlier than 1991 since there were major changes in methodology in 1991. These changes were made to improve accuracy in the estimates.

Coverage of an Individual Table

Since the Survey covers many activities in various places by participants of different ages, all table titles, headnotes, stubs, and footnotes are designed to identify and articulate each item being reported in the table. For example, the title of Table 2 shows that data about anglers and hunters, their days of participation, and their number of trips are reported by type of activity. By contrast, the title of Table 7 indicates that it contains data on freshwater anglers and the days they fished for different species.

Percentages Reported in the Tables

Percentages are reported in the tables for the convenience of the user. When exclusive groups are being reported, the base of a percentage is apparent from its context because the percents add to 100 percent (plus or minus a rounding error). For example, Table 2 reports the number of trips taken by big game hunters, those taken by small game hunters, those taken by migratory bird hunters, and those taken by hunters pursuing other animals. These comprise 100 percent because they are exclusive categories.

Percents should not add to 100 when nonexclusive groups are being reported. Using Table 2 as an example again, note that adding the percentages associated with the total number of big game hunters, total small game hunters, total migratory bird hunters, and total hunters of other animals will not yield total hunters because respondents could hunt for more than one type of game.

When the base of the percentage is not apparent in context, it is identified in a footnote. For example, Table 15 reports two percentages with different bases: one base being the number of total participants at the head of the column and the other base being the total population who are described by the row category. Footnotes are used to clarify the bases of the reported percentages.

Footnotes to the Tables

Footnotes are used to clarify the information or items that are being reported in a table. Symbols in the body of a table indicate important footnotes. These symbols are used in the tables to refer to the same footnote each time they appear:

* Estimate based on a sample size of 10–29.

... Sample size too small to report data reliably because there were fewer than 10 responses.

W Less than .5 dollars.

Z Less than 0.5 percent.

X Not applicable.

NA Not asked.

Estimates based upon fewer than 10 responses are regarded as being based on a sample size that is too small for reliable reporting. An estimate based upon at least 10 but fewer than 30 responses is treated as an estimate based on a small sample size. Other footnotes appear, as necessary, to qualify or clarify the estimates reported in the tables. In addition, these two important footnotes appear frequently:

• Detail does not add to total because of multiple responses.

• Detail does not add to total because of multiple responses and nonresponse.

"Multiple responses" is a term used to reflect the fact that individuals or their characteristics fall into more than one category. Using Table 12 as an example, those who hunt for big game, small game, migratory birds, and other animals are counted only once as a hunter in the "Total, all hunting" row. Another example is Table 15, where total anglers and hunters add up to more than total sportspersons. Totals will be smaller than the sum of subcategories when multiple responses exist.

"Nonresponse" exists because the Survey questions were answered voluntarily and some respondents did not or could not answer all the questions. Totals are greater than the sum of subcategories when nonresponses have occurred. This occurs because some respondents answered the question that provided the category estimate but did not answer the subcategory questions.

Table 1. Fishing and Hunting in Louisiana by Resident and Nonresident Sportspersons: 2006

(Population 16 years old and older. Numbers in thousands)

Sportspersons	Total, state residents and nonresidents		State residents		Nonresidents	
	Number	Percent of sportspersons	Number	Percent of resident sportspersons	Number	Percent of nonresident sportspersons
Total sportspersons (fished or hunted)	769	100	651	100	119	100
Total anglers	702	91	590	91	112	94
Fished only.............................	499	65	410	63	*89	*75
Fished and hunted	203	26	180	28	...	...
Total hunters............................	270	35	241	37	...	...
Hunted only	*68	*9	*61	*9	...	...
Hunted and fished	203	26	180	28	...	...

* Estimate based on a sample size of 10–29.   ... Sample size too small to report data reliably.

Note: Detail does not add to total because of multiple responses.

Table 2. Anglers and Hunters, Days of Participation, and Trips in Louisiana by Type of Fishing and Hunting: 2006

(Population 16 years old and older. Numbers in thousands)

Type of fishing and hunting	Participants		Days of participation		Trips	
	Number	Percent	Number	Percent	Number	Percent
FISHING						
Total, all fishing	702	100	11,204	100	9,150	100
Total, all freshwater......................	549	78	8,743	78	6,823	75
Freshwater, except Great Lakes............	549	78	8,743	78	6,823	75
Great Lakes	...	...	...	...	...	...
Saltwater.............................	289	41	2,975	27	2,327	25
HUNTING						
Total, all hunting	270	100	5,979	100	5,815	100
Big game	204	76	4,013	67	2,883	50
Small game.............................	126	47	1,447	24	1,407	24
Migratory bird	100	37	1,419	24	1,286	22
Other animals...........................	*32	*12	*487	*8	*238	*4

* Estimate based on a sample size of 10–29.   ... Sample size too small to report data reliably.

Note: Detail does not add to total because of multiple responses.

Table 3. Anglers and Hunters, Trips, and Days of Participation: 2006

(Population 16 years old and older. Numbers in thousands)

Anglers and hunters, trips, and days of participation	Activity in Louisiana						Activity by Louisiana residents in United States					
	Total, state residents and nonresidents		State residents		Nonresidents		Total, in state of residence and in other states		In state of residence		In other states	
	Number	Percent	Number	Percent	Number	Percent	Number	Percent	Number	Percent	Number	Percent
FISHING												
Total anglers	702	100	590	84	112	16	598	100	590	99	*64	*11
Total trips	9,150	100	8,815	96	335	4	9,133	100	8,815	97	*318	*3
Total days of fishing.........	11,204	100	10,564	94	640	6	11,075	100	10,564	95	*641	*6
Average days of fishing	16	(X)	18	(X)	6	(X)	19	(X)	18	(X)	*10	(X)
HUNTING												
Total hunters	270	100	241	89	...	...	275	100	241	87	*75	*27
Total trips	5,815	100	5,764	99	...	...	6,613	100	5,764	87	*849	*13
Total days of hunting	5,979	100	5,847	98	...	...	7,155	100	5,847	82	*1,431	*20
Average days of hunting	22	(X)	24	(X)	...	(X)	26	(X)	24	(X)	*19	(X)

(X) Not applicable.   * Estimate based on a sample size of 10–29.   ... Sample size too small to report data reliably.

Note: Detail does not add to total because of multiple responses.

Table 4. Louisiana Resident Anglers and Hunters by Place Fished or Hunted: 2006

(State population 16 years old and older. Numbers in thousands)

Place fished or hunted	Anglers		Hunters	
	Number	Percent	Number	Percent
Total, all places..	**598**	**100**	**275**	**100**
In-state only...	534	89	200	73
In-state and other states...............................	*56	*9	*40	*15
In other states only	...	...	*35	*13

* Estimate based on a sample size of 10–29.   ... Sample size too small to report data reliably.

Note: Detail may not add to total because of multiple responses and nonresponse.

Table 5. Louisiana Resident Anglers and Hunters, Days of Participation, and Trips in the United States by Type of Fishing and Hunting: 2006

(State population 16 years old and older. Numbers in thousands)

Type of fishing and hunting	Participants		Days of participation		Trips	
	Number	Percent	Number	Percent	Number	Percent
FISHING						
Total, all fishing	**598**	**100**	**11,075**	**100**	**9,133**	**100**
Total, all freshwater.......................	483	81	8,791	79	6,922	76
Freshwater, except Great Lakes.............	483	81	8,791	79	6,920	76
Great Lakes	...	...	...	...	...	...
Saltwater.................................	261	44	2,601	23	2,211	24
HUNTING						
Total, all hunting	**275**	**100**	**7,155**	**100**	**6,613**	**100**
Big game	217	79	5,002	70	3,493	53
Small game..............................	142	52	1,687	24	1,531	23
Migratory bird	97	35	1,420	20	1,345	20
Other animals...........................	*34	*12	*496	*7	*244	*4

* Estimate based on a sample size of 10–29.　　... Sample size too small to report data reliably.

Note: Detail does not add to total because of multiple responses.

Table 6. Freshwater Anglers, Trips, Days of Fishing, and Type of Water Fished: 2006

(Population 16 years old and older. Numbers in thousands)

Anglers, trips, and days of fishing	Activity in Louisiana					
	Total, state residents and nonresidents		State residents		Nonresidents	
	Number	Percent	Number	Percent	Number	Percent
Total anglers..............................	**549**	**100**	**472**	**86**	***77**	***14**
Total trips	**6,823**	**100**	**6,659**	**98**	***164**	***2**
Total days of fishing.......................	**8,743**	**100**	**8,312**	**95**	***431**	***5**
Average days of fishing.....................	16	(X)	18	(X)	*6	(X)
ANGLERS						
Total, all types of water....................	**549**	**100**	**472**	**86**	***77**	***14**
Ponds, lakes, or reservoirs.................	471	100	406	86	*65	*14
Rivers or streams	240	100	220	92	...	...
DAYS						
Total, all types of water....................	**8,743**	**100**	**8,312**	**95**	***431**	***5**
Ponds, lakes, or reservoirs.................	6,296	100	6,108	97	*188	*3
Rivers or streams	3,161	100	3,002	95	...	...

* Estimate based on a sample size of 10–29.　　... Sample size too small to report data reliably.　　(X) Not applicable.

Note: Detail does not add to total because of multiple responses.

Table 7. Freshwater Anglers and Days of Fishing in Louisiana by Type of Fish: 2006

(Population 16 years old and older. Numbers in thousands)

Anglers and days of fishing	Activity in Louisiana						
	Total, state residents and nonresidents			State residents		Nonresidents	
	Number	Percent of total types	Percent of anglers/ days	Number	Percent of anglers/ days	Number	Percent of anglers/ days
ANGLERS							
Total, all types of fish	**549**	**100**	**100**	472	86	*77	*14
Crappie.........................	148	27	100	127	86	...	...
Panfish	215	39	100	206	96	...	...
White bass, striped bass, striped bass hybrids	159	29	100	132	83	...	...
Black bass	187	34	100	146	78	...	...
Catfish, bullheads........................	207	38	100	201	97	...	...
Walleye, sauger	...	...	...	...	...	...	...
Northern pike, pickerel, muskie, muskie hybrids...	...	...	...	...	...	...	...
Steelhead	...	...	...	...	...	...	...
Trout..........................	*72	*13	*100	*55	*76	...	...
Salmon	...	...	...	...	...	...	...
Anything[1]......................	*67	*12	*100	*65	*96	...	...
Other freshwater fish	*81	*15	*100	*72	*89	...	...
DAYS							
Total, all types of fish	**8,743**	**100**	**100**	8,312	95	*431	*5
Crappie.........................	2,377	27	100	2,341	98	...	...
Panfish	3,642	42	100	3,600	99	...	...
White bass, striped bass, striped bass hybrids	2,138	24	100	2,073	97	...	...
Black bass	3,193	37	100	3,101	97	...	...
Catfish, bullheads........................	2,433	28	100	2,399	99	...	...
Walleye, sauger	...	...	...	...	...	...	...
Northern pike, pickerel, muskie, muskie hybrids...	...	...	...	...	...	...	...
Steelhead	...	...	...	...	...	...	...
Trout..........................	*881	*10	*100	*829	*94	...	...
Salmon	...	...	...	...	...	...	...
Anything[1]......................	*537	*6	*100	*534	*100	...	...
Other freshwater fish	*1,556	*18	*100	*1,538	*99	...	...

* Estimate based on a sample size of 10–29.   ... Sample size too small to report data reliably.

[1] Respondent fished for no specific species and identified "Anything" from a list of categories of fish.

Note: Detail does not add to total because of multiple responses.

Table 8. Great Lakes Anglers, Trips, and Days of Fishing in Louisiana: 2006

This table does not apply to this state.

Table 9. Great Lakes Anglers and Days of Fishing in Louisiana by Type of Fish: 2006

This table does not apply to this state.

Table 10. Saltwater Anglers, Trips, and Days of Fishing in Louisiana: 2006

(Population 16 years old and older. Numbers in thousands)

Anglers, trips, and days of fishing	Activity in Louisiana					
	Total, state residents and nonresidents		State residents		Nonresidents	
	Number	Percent	Number	Percent	Number	Percent
Total anglers............................	289	100	248	86	*42	*14
Total trips..............................	2,327	100	2,156	93	*171	*7
Total days..............................	2,975	100	2,541	85	*433	*15
Average days of fishing....................	10	(X)	10	(X)	*10	(X)

* Estimate based on a sample size of 10–29.   (X) Not applicable.

Note: Detail does not add to total because of multiple responses.

Table 11. Saltwater Anglers and Days of Fishing in Louisiana by Type of Fish: 2006

(Population 16 years old and older. Numbers in thousands)

Anglers and days of fishing	Activity in Louisiana					
	Total, state residents and nonresidents			State residents		Nonresidents	
	Number	Percent of total types	Percent of anglers/ days	Number	Percent of anglers/ days	Number	Percent of anglers/ days
ANGLERS							
Total, all types of fish	**289**	**100**	**100**	**248**	**86**	***42**	***14**
Salmon............................	...	...	...	...	...	...	...
Striped bass	...	...	...	...	...	...	...
Bluefish	...	...	...	...	...	...	...
Flatfish (flounder, halibut).............	*61	*21	*100	*49	*81	...	...
Red drum (redfish)	196	68	100	170	87	*26	*13
Sea trout (weakfish)...................	100	34	100	84	84	...	...
Mackerel...........................	...	...	...	...	...	...	...
Mahi-mahi	...	...	...	...	...	...	...
Shellfish	...	...	...	...	...	...	...
Anything[1]...........................	*65	*22	*100	*55	*86	...	...
Other saltwater fish	*72	*25	*100	*59	*82	...	...
DAYS							
Total, all types of fish	**2,975**	**100**	**100**	**2,541**	**85**	***433**	***15**
Salmon............................	...	...	...	...	...	...	...
Striped bass	...	...	...	...	...	...	...
Bluefish	...	...	...	...	...	...	...
Flatfish (flounder, halibut).............	*713	*24	*100	*681	*95	...	...
Red drum (redfish)	2,124	71	100	1,777	84	*347	*16
Sea trout (weakfish)...................	1,341	45	100	1,046	78	...	...
Mackerel...........................	...	...	...	...	...	...	...
Mahi-mahi	...	...	...	...	...	...	...
Shellfish	...	...	...	...	...	...	...
Anything[1]...........................	*363	*12	*100	*333	*92	...	...
Other saltwater fish	*567	*19	*100	*477	*84	...	...

* Estimate based on a sample size of 10–29.   ... Sample size too small to report data reliably.

[1] Respondent fished for no specific species and identified "Anything" from a list of categories of fish.

Note: Detail does not add to total because of multiple responses.

Table 12. **Hunters, Trips, and Days of Hunting in Louisiana by Type of Hunting: 2006**

(Population 16 years old and older. Numbers in thousands)

Hunters, trips, and days of hunting	Activity in Louisiana					
	Total, state residents and nonresidents		State residents		Nonresidents	
	Number	Percent	Number	Percent	Number	Percent
HUNTERS						
Total, all hunting	**270**	**100**	**241**	**89**	...	...
Big game	204	100	182	89	...	...
Small game............................	126	100	126	100	...	...
Migratory bird	100	100	93	93	...	...
Other animals.........................	*32	*100	*32	*100	...	...
TRIPS						
Total, all hunting	**5,815**	**100**	**5,764**	**99**	...	...
Big game	2,883	100	2,851	99	...	...
Small game............................	1,407	100	1,407	100	...	...
Migratory bird	1,286	100	1,268	99	...	...
Other animals.........................	*238	*100	*238	*100	...	...
DAYS						
Total, all hunting	**5,979**	**100**	**5,847**	**98**	...	...
Big game	4,013	100	3,918	98	...	...
Small game............................	1,447	100	1,447	100	...	...
Migratory bird	1,419	100	1,382	97	...	...
Other animals.........................	*487	*100	*487	*100	...	...

* Estimate based on a sample size of 10–29.   ... Sample size too small to report data reliably.

Note: Detail does not add to total because of multiple responses.

Table 13. Hunters and Days of Hunting in Louisiana by Type of Game: 2006

(Population 16 years old and older. Numbers in thousands)

Type of game	Hunters, state residents and nonresidents		Days of hunting	
	Number	Percent	Number	Percent
Total, all types of game	270	100	5,979	100
Big game, total	204	76	4,013	67
Deer	202	75	3,508	59
Elk	...	...	...	...
Bear	...	...	...	...
Wild turkey......................................	*47	*17	*552	*9
Other big game	...	...	...	...
Small game, total	126	47	1,447	24
Rabbit, hare	*86	*32	*949	*16
Quail..	...	...	...	...
Grouse/prairie chicken...........................	...	...	...	...
Squirrel...	90	33	1,066	18
Pheasant	...	...	...	...
Other small game................................	...	...	...	...
Migratory birds, total	100	37	1,419	24
Waterfowl.......................................	74	27	1,126	19
Geese	...	...	...	...
Duck	*72	*27	*1,191	*20
Dove	*38	*14	*141	*2
Other migratory bird	...	...	...	...
Other animals, total [1]	*32	*12	*487	*8

* Estimate based on a sample size of 10–29.   ... Sample size too small to report data reliably.

[1] Includes groundhog, raccoon, fox, coyote, crow, prairie dog, etc.

Note: Detail does not add to total because of multiple responses.

Table 14. Hunters and Days of Hunting in Louisiana by Type of Land: 2006

(Population 16 years old and older. Numbers in thousands)

Hunters and days of hunting	Total, state residents and nonresidents		State residents		Nonresidents	
	Number	Percent	Number	Percent	Number	Percent
HUNTERS						
Total, all types of land.....................	270	100	241	100	...	...
Public land, total	*59	*22	*56	*23	...	...
Public land only...........................	...	...	...	...	...	...
Public and private land	*47	*17	*43	*18	...	...
Private land, total........................	235	87	205	85	...	...
Private land only	188	69	162	67	...	...
Private and public land	*47	*17	*43	*18	...	...
DAYS						
Total, all types of land.....................	5,979	100	5,847	100	...	...
Public land[1]	*819	*14	*807	*14	...	...
Private land[2].............................	5,512	92	5,407	92	...	...

* Estimate based on a sample size of 10–29.   ... Sample size too small to report data reliably.

[1] Days of hunting on public land includes both days spent solely on public land and those spent on public and private land.
[2] Days of hunting on private land includes both days spent solely on private land and those spent on private and public land.

Note: Detail does not add to total because of multiple responses and nonresponse.

Table 15. Selected Characteristics of Louisiana Resident Anglers and Hunters: 2006

(State population 16 years old and older. Numbers in thousands)

Characteristic	Population		Sportspersons (fished or hunted)				Anglers			Hunters		
	Number	Percent	Number	Percent who partici-pated	Percent of sports-persons		Number	Percent who partici-pated	Percent of anglers	Number	Percent who partici-pated	Percent of hunters
Total persons.....................	**3,433**	**100**	**678**	**20**	**100**		**598**	**17**	**100**	**275**	**8**	**100**
Population Density of Residence												
Urban	2,322	68	356	15	52		318	14	53	127	5	46
Rural.........................	1,110	32	322	29	48		280	25	47	149	13	54
Population Size of Residence												
Metropolitan statistical area												
(MSA).....................	3,008	88	563	19	83		494	16	83	212	7	77
1,000,000 or more	768	22	117	15	17		100	13	17	*43	*6	*16
250,000 to 999,999	1,000	29	180	18	27		164	16	27	*75	*7	*27
Less than 250,000	1,239	36	266	21	39		230	19	39	94	8	34
Outside MSA	425	12	115	27	17		104	24	17	*64	*15	*23
Sex												
Male	1,613	47	505	31	74		428	27	72	260	16	95
Female	1,820	53	174	10	26		170	9	28	...	...	...
Age												
16 to 17 years	126	4	...	...	...		...	...	...	...	...	...
18 to 24 years	347	10	*55	*16	*8		*45	*13	*8	*40	*11	*14
25 to 34 years	526	15	90	17	13		*80	*15	*13	*39	*7	*14
35 to 44 years	599	17	183	31	27		163	27	27	*66	*11	*24
45 to 54 years	647	19	122	19	18		115	18	19	*46	*7	*17
55 to 64 years	547	16	136	25	20		127	23	21	*42	*8	*15
65 years and older	642	19	*75	*12	*11		*50	*8	*8	*37	*6	*14
Ethnicity												
Hispanic	77	2	...	...	...		...	...	...	...	...	...
Non-Hispanic	3,356	98	660	20	97		579	17	97	275	8	100
Race												
White	2,343	68	553	24	82		493	21	82	229	10	83
Black.........................	1,017	30	120	12	18		*103	*10	*17	*43	*4	*16
All others	73	2	...	...	...		...	...	...	...	...	...
Annual Household Income												
Under $10,000	329	10	*60	*18	*9		*60	*18	*10	...	...	...
$10,000 to $19,999	313	9	...	...	...		...	...	...	...	...	...
$20,000 to $29,999	329	10	*52	*16	*8		*50	*15	*8	...	...	...
$30,000 to $39,999	362	11	*67	*18	*10		*60	*17	*10	*34	*9	*12
$40,000 to $49,999	256	7	93	36	14		*80	*31	*13	*28	*11	*10
$50,000 to $74,999	479	14	131	27	19		111	23	18	*58	*12	*21
$75,000 to $99,999	317	9	94	30	14		80	25	13	*42	*13	*15
$100,000 or more..............	163	5	78	48	12		70	43	12	*44	*27	*16
Not reported	885	26	83	9	12		67	8	11	...	...	...
Education												
11 years or less	666	19	115	17	17		109	16	18	*42	*6	*15
12 years	1,338	39	281	21	41		245	18	41	106	8	38
1 to 3 years college	725	21	152	21	22		129	18	22	*64	*9	*23
4 years college or more..........	703	20	131	19	19		115	16	19	*64	*9	*23

* Estimate based on a sample size of 10–29.   ... Sample size too small to report data reliably.

Note: Detail does not add to total because of multiple responses. Percent who participated shows the percent of each row's population who participated in the activity named by the column (the percent of those living in urban areas who fished, etc.). Remaining percent columns show the percent of each column's participants who are described by the row heading (the percent of anglers who lived in urban areas, etc.).

Table 16. Summary of Expenditures in Louisiana by State Residents and Nonresidents Combined for Fishing and Hunting: 2006

(Population 16 years old and older)

Expenditure item	Amount (thousands of dollars)	Spenders (thousands)	Average per spender (dollars)	Average per sportsperson (dollars)
FISHING AND HUNTING				
Total..	**1,711,229**	**747**	**2,291**	**2,199**
Food and lodging..................................	180,224	601	300	234
Transportation..................................	160,672	561	286	209
Other trip costs[1]	201,822	564	358	262
Equipment (fishing, hunting)......................	256,457	497	516	310
Auxiliary equipment[2]............................	67,185	161	417	86
Special equipment[3]..............................	477,742	91	5,239	620
Magazines and books.............................	5,991	140	43	8
Membership dues and contributions	22,617	89	255	29
Other[4]	338,519	458	740	440
FISHING				
Total..	**1,006,136**	**650**	**1,548**	**1,416**
Food and lodging..................................	96,927	535	181	138
Transportation..................................	87,043	473	184	124
Other trip costs[1]	153,393	533	288	219
Fishing equipment	122,194	411	297	156
Auxiliary equipment[2]............................	*7,633	*38	*200	*11
Special equipment[3]..............................	*294,738	*45	*6,597	*420
Magazines and books.............................	*1,622	*39	*42	*2
Membership dues and contributions	*1,029	*28	*36	*1
Other[4]	241,557	333	726	344
HUNTING				
Total..	**525,505**	**283**	**1,859**	**1,904**
Food and lodging..................................	83,297	216	386	308
Transportation..................................	73,628	199	369	272
Other trip costs[1]	48,429	109	443	179
Hunting equipment................................	114,697	193	596	391
Auxiliary equipment[2]............................	23,285	88	264	86
Special equipment[3]..............................	...	...	...	...
Magazines and books.............................	*2,386	*36	*66	*9
Membership dues and contributions	*14,731	*34	*430	*53
Other[4]	96,962	180	539	354
UNSPECIFIED[5]				
Total..	**160,023**	**114**	**1,398**	**206**

* Estimate based on a sample size of 10–29.　　　... Sample size too small to report data reliably.

[1] Includes boating costs, equipment rental, guide fees, access fees, heating and cooking fuel, and ice and bait (for fishing only).
[2] Includes tents, special clothing, etc.
[3] Includes boats, campers, 4x4 vehicles, cabins, etc.
[4] Includes land leasing and ownership, licenses, stamps, tags, and permits.
[5] Respondent could not specify whether expenditure was primarily for either fishing or hunting.

Note: Detail does not add to total because of multiple responses and nonresponse. See Tables 19–20 for a detailed listing of expenditure items.

Table 17. **Summary of Fishing Trip and Equipment Expenditures in Louisiana by State Residents and Nonresidents Combined by Type of Fishing: 2006**

(Population 16 years old and older)

Expenditure item	Amount (thousands of dollars)	Spenders (thousands)	Average per spender (dollars)	Average per angler (dollars)
ALL FISHING				
Total........................	**761,927**	**625**	**1,220**	**1,068**
Food and lodging.............	96,927	535	181	138
Transportation................	87,043	473	184	124
Other trip costs...............	153,393	533	288	219
Equipment	424,564	418	1,016	587
ALL FRESHWATER				
Total........................	**404,569**	**488**	**830**	**733**
Food and lodging.............	60,208	414	145	110
Transportation................	54,691	352	156	100
Other trip costs...............	86,930	427	204	158
Equipment	202,740	265	766	365
FRESHWATER, EXCEPT GREAT LAKES				
Total........................	**403,899**	**488**	**828**	**732**
Food and lodging.............	60,208	414	145	110
Transportation................	54,021	352	154	98
Other trip costs...............	86,930	427	204	158
Equipment	202,740	265	766	365
GREAT LAKES				
Total........................	...	...	...	...
Food and lodging.............	...	...	...	...
Transportation................	...	...	...	...
Other trip costs...............	...	...	...	...
Equipment	...	...	...	...
SALTWATER				
Total........................	**336,943**	**242**	**1,390**	**1,128**
Food and lodging.............	36,719	221	166	127
Transportation................	32,352	199	163	112
Other trip costs...............	66,463	206	323	230
Equipment	201,409	140	1,439	660

... Sample size too small to report data reliably.

Note: Detail does not add to total because of multiple responses and nonresponse. See Table 19 for detailed listing of expenditure items.

Table 18. Summary of Hunting Trip and Equipment Expenditures in Louisiana by State Residents and Nonresidents Combined by Type of Hunting: 2006

(Population 16 years old and older)

Expenditure item	Amount (thousands of dollars)	Spenders (thousands)	Average per spender (dollars)	Average per hunter (dollars)
ALL HUNTING				
Total............................	**411,426**	**262**	**1,568**	**1,488**
Food and lodging................	83,297	216	386	308
Transportation..................	73,628	199	369	272
Other trip costs................	48,429	109	443	179
Equipment	206,072	204	1,009	729
BIG GAME				
Total............................	**286,233**	**216**	**1,328**	**1,346**
Food and lodging................	60,488	170	356	296
Transportation..................	53,045	154	344	259
Other trip costs................	34,278	74	465	168
Equipment	138,422	152	913	623
SMALL GAME				
Total............................	**35,602**	**96**	**370**	**844**
Food and lodging................	6,161	75	83	270
Transportation..................	*7,221	*57	*126	*317
Other trip costs................	*3,806	*28	*135	*167
Equipment	*18,414	*53	*345	*90
MIGRATORY BIRD				
Total............................	**58,883**	**82**	**718**	**1,699**
Food and lodging................	16,121	76	212	555
Transportation..................	12,898	74	174	444
Other trip costs................	*9,716	*31	*313	*334
Equipment	*20,149	*39	*514	*366
OTHER ANIMALS				
Total............................	...	...	...	...
Food and lodging................	...	...	...	...
Transportation..................	...	...	...	...
Other trip costs................	...	...	...	...
Equipment	...	...	...	...

* Estimate based on a sample size of 10–29.   ... Sample size too small to report data reliably.

Note: Detail does not add to total because of multiple responses and nonresponse. See Table 20 for detailed listing of expenditure items.

Table 19. Expenditures in Louisiana by State Residents and Nonresidents Combined for Fishing: 2006

(Population 16 years old and older)

Expenditure item	Expenditures		Spenders		
	Amount (thousands of dollars)	Average per angler (dollars)	Number (thousands)	Percent of anglers	Average per spender (dollars)
Total, all items.................................	1,006,136	1,416	650	93	1,548
TRIP-RELATED EXPENDITURES					
Total trip-related.............................	337,363	481	588	84	574
Food and lodging, total	96,927	138	557	79	174
Food	84,624	121	532	76	159
Lodging......................................	12,303	18	66	9	186
Transportation..................................	87,043	124	473	67	184
Other trip costs, total...........................	153,393	219	533	76	288
Privilege and other fees[1]	22,905	33	146	21	156
Boating costs[2]................................	81,971	117	210	30	390
Bait	34,118	49	438	62	78
Ice	12,870	18	392	56	33
Heating and cooking fuel......................	*1,530	*2	*47	*7	*33
EQUIPMENT AND OTHER EXPENDITURES PRIMARILY FOR FISHING					
Fishing equipment, total	122,194	156	411	59	297
Reels, rods, and rod-making components	46,000	64	259	37	178
Lines, hooks, sinkers, etc.	21,959	31	344	49	64
Artificial lures and flies......................	18,568	25	275	39	67
Creels, stringers, fish bags, landing nets, and gaff hooks..	2,865	4	72	10	40
Minnow seines, traps, and bait containers.	*2,888	*4	*59	*8	*49
Other fishing equipment[3]	29,914	28	156	22	192
Auxiliary equipment[4]	*7,633	*11	*38	*5	*200
Special equipment[5].............................	*294,738	*420	*45	*6	*6,597
Other fishing costs[6]	244,208	348	349	50	699

* Estimate based on a sample size of 10–29.

[1] Includes boat or equipment rental and fees for guides, pack trip (party and charter boats, etc.), public land use, and private land use.
[2] Boat launching, mooring, storage, maintenance, insurance, pumpout fees, and fuel.
[3] Includes electronic fishing devices (depth finders, fish finders, etc.), tackle boxes, ice fishing equipment, and other fishing equipment.
[4] Includes tents, special fishing clothing, etc.
[5] Includes boats, campers, 4x4 vehicles, cabins, etc.
[6] Includes magazines and books, membership dues and contributions, land leasing and ownership, and licenses, stamps, tags, and permits.

Note: Detail does not add to total because of multiple responses and nonresponse. Percent of anglers may be greater than 100 because spenders who did not fish in this state are included.

Table 20. Expenditures in Louisiana by State Residents and Nonresidents Combined for Hunting: 2006

(Population 16 years old and older)

Expenditure item	Expenditures		Spenders		
	Amount (thousands of dollars)	Average per hunter (dollars)	Number (thousands)	Percent of hunters	Average per spender (dollars)
Total, all items................................	**525,505**	**1,904**	**283**	**104**	**1,859**
TRIP-RELATED EXPENDITURES					
Total trip-related.............................	**205,355**	**759**	**222**	**82**	**926**
Food and lodging, total	**83,297**	**308**	**222**	**82**	**376**
Food	68,804	254	213	79	323
Lodging.....................................	*14,493	*54	*32	*12	*450
Transportation.................................	73,628	272	199	74	369
Other trip costs, total.........................	**48,429**	**179**	**109**	**40**	**443**
Privilege and other fees[1]	*29,417	*109	*78	*29	*377
Boating costs...............................	*13,516	*50	*44	*16	*306
Heating and cooking fuel......................	...	...	...	...	...
EQUIPMENT AND OTHER EXPENDITURES PRIMARILY FOR HUNTING					
Hunting equipment, total........................	**114,697**	**391**	**193**	**71**	**596**
Firearms	60,536	199	98	36	617
Ammunition	14,088	51	167	62	84
Other hunting equipment[2]	40,073	141	108	40	369
Auxiliary equipment[3]	23,285	86	88	33	264
Special equipment[4].............................	...	...	...	...	...
Other hunting costs[5]............................	114,078	416	195	72	584

* Estimate based on a sample size of 10–29.   ... Sample size too small to report data reliably.

[1] Includes guide fees, pack trip or package fees, public and private land use access fees, and rental of equipment such as boats and hunting or camping equipment.
[2] Includes bows, arrows, archery equipment, telescopic sights, decoys and game calls, handloading equipment and components, hunting dogs and associated costs, hunting knives, and other hunting equipment.
[3] Includes tents, special hunting clothing, etc.
[4] Includes boats, campers, 4x4 vehicles, cabins, etc.
[5] Includes magazines and books, membership dues and contributions, land leasing and ownership, and licenses, stamps, and permits.

Note: Detail does not add to total because of multiple responses and nonresponse. Percent of hunters may be greater than 100 percent because spenders who did not hunt in this state are included.

Table 21. Trip and Equipment Expenditures in Louisiana for Fishing and Hunting by Louisiana Residents and Nonresidents: 2006

(Population 16 years old and older)

Expenditure item	Amount (thousands of dollars)	Spenders (thousands)	Average per spender (dollars)	Average per sportsperson (dollars)
STATE RESIDENTS AND NONRESIDENTS				
Trip and equipment expenditures for fishing and hunting, total	1,301,562	701	1,858	1,692
Trip and equipment expenditures for fishing, total	761,927	625	1,220	1,086
Food and lodging....................................	96,927	535	181	138
Transportation.	87,043	473	184	124
Boating costs[1].....................................	81,971	210	390	117
Other trip costs[2]..................................	71,421	531	134	102
Equipment	424,564	418	1,016	605
Trip and equipment expenditures for hunting, total	411,426	262	1,568	1,521
Food and lodging....................................	83,297	216	386	308
Transportation.	73,628	199	369	272
Boating costs[1].....................................	*13,516	*44	*306	*50
Other trip costs[2]..................................	34,914	95	367	129
Equipment	206,072	204	1,009	762
Unspecified equipment[3]...............................	128,209	43	3,012	167
STATE RESIDENTS				
Trip and equipment expenditures for fishing and hunting, total	1,115,224	585	1,907	1,714
Trip and equipment expenditures for fishing, total	592,265	521	1,136	1,004
Food and lodging....................................	71,952	441	163	122
Transportation.	63,833	385	166	108
Boating costs[1].....................................	72,817	187	390	123
Other trip costs[2]..................................	50,326	453	111	85
Equipment	333,335	388	859	565
Trip and equipment expenditures for hunting, total	396,434	226	1,755	1,646
Food and lodging....................................	76,951	187	412	319
Transportation.	69,791	175	399	290
Boating costs[1].....................................	*12,743	*40	*315	*53
Other trip costs[2]..................................	33,880	89	381	141
Equipment	203,070	197	1,033	843
Unspecified equipment[3]...............................	*126,525	*38	*3,336	*194
NONRESIDENTS				
Trip and equipment expenditures for fishing and hunting, total	186,339	116	1,608	1,572
Trip and equipment expenditures for fishing, total	169,663	103	1,641	1,520
Food and lodging....................................	24,975	94	266	224
Transportation.	*23,210	*89	*262	*208
Boating costs[1].....................................	*9,154	*23	*390	*82
Other trip costs[2]..................................	*21,095	*78	*270	*189
Equipment	*91,229	*30	*3,057	*817
Trip and equipment expenditures for hunting, total	*14,992	*36	*411	*506
Food and lodging....................................	...	...	...	...
Transportation.	...	...	...	...
Boating costs[1].....................................	...	...	...	...
Other trip costs[2]..................................	...	...	...	...
Equipment	...	...	...	...
Unspecified equipment[3]...............................	...	...	...	...

* Estimate based on a sample size of 10–29.   ... Sample size too small to report data reliably.

[1] Includes boat launching, mooring, storage, maintenance, insurance, pumpout fees, and fuel.
[2] Includes equipment rental, guide and access fees, ice and bait for fishing, and heating and cooking oil.
[3] Respondent could not specify whether item was for hunting or fishing.

Note: Detail does not add to total because of multiple responses and nonresponse.

Table 22. Summary of Louisiana Residents' Fishing and Hunting Expenditures Both Inside and Outside Louisiana: 2006

(State population 16 years old and older)

Expenditure item	Amount (thousands of dollars)	Spenders (thousands)	Average per spender (dollars)	Average per sportsperson (dollars)
FISHING AND HUNTING				
Total..	**1,602,726**	**644**	**2,490**	**2,362**
Food and lodging............................	188,119	531	354	277
Transportation..............................	163,532	503	325	241
Other trip costs[1].........................	211,642	506	418	312
Equipment (fishing, hunting)................	264,841	469	565	390
Auxiliary equipment[2]......................	66,680	165	403	98
Special equipment[3]........................	410,860	88	4,643	606
Magazines and books........................	6,659	146	45	10
Membership dues and contributions	26,162	95	277	39
Other[4]....................................	264,232	416	634	389
FISHING				
Total..	**807,063**	**553**	**1,459**	**1,350**
Food and lodging............................	88,009	454	194	147
Transportation..............................	70,716	398	178	118
Other trip costs[1].........................	130,706	466	280	219
Fishing equipment..........................	118,947	386	308	199
Auxiliary equipment[2]......................	*4,469	*34	*132	*7
Special equipment[3]........................	*228,641	*45	*5,067	*382
Magazines and books........................	*1,955	*42	*46	*3
Membership dues and contributions	*860	*23	*38	*1
Other[4]....................................	162,761	287	568	272
HUNTING				
Total..	**618,264**	**258**	**2,396**	**2,244**
Food and lodging............................	100,110	221	454	363
Transportation..............................	92,817	211	440	337
Other trip costs[1].........................	80,936	118	686	294
Hunting equipment..........................	126,328	188	671	459
Auxiliary equipment[2]......................	26,766	99	270	97
Special equipment[3]........................	...	...	...	...
Magazines and books........................	*2,731	*43	*63	*10
Membership dues and contributions	*19,016	*43	*440	*69
Other[4]....................................	101,470	186	544	368
UNSPECIFIED[5]				
Total..	**157,833**	**106**	**1,482**	**233**

* Estimate based on a sample size of 10–29.   ... Sample size too small to report data reliably.

[1] Includes boating costs, equipment rental, guide fees, access fees, heating and cooking fuel, and ice and bait (for fishing only).
[2] Includes tents, special clothing, etc.
[3] Includes boats, campers, 4x4 vehicles, cabins, etc.
[4] Includes land leasing and ownership, licenses, stamps, tags, and permits.
[5] Respondent could not specify whether expenditure was primarily for either fishing or hunting.

Note: Detail does not add to total because of multiple responses and nonresponse. See Tables 19–20 for a detailed listing of expenditure items.

Table 23. In-State and Out-of-State Expenditures by Louisiana Residents for Fishing and Hunting: 2006

(State population 16 years old and older)

Expenditure item	Amount (thousands of dollars)	Spenders (thousands)	Average per spender (dollars)	Average per sportsperson (dollars)
IN LOUISIANA				
Expenditures for fishing and hunting, total	**1,421,937**	**630**	**2,258**	**2,185**
Trip-related expenditures	452,294	550	823	695
Equipment (fishing and hunting)........................	239,441	464	516	368
Auxiliary equipment[1]................................	62,764	151	417	96
Special equipment[2].................................	*403,263	*87	*4,651	*620
Other[3]	264,174	434	609	406
Expenditures for fishing, total	**756,799**	**546**	**1,387**	**1,283**
Trip-related expenditures	258,929	494	525	439
Fishing equipment	108,179	382	283	183
Auxiliary equipment[1]................................	*4,111	*32	*128	*7
Special equipment[2].................................	*221,045	*43	*5,101	*375
Other[3]	164,534	298	552	279
Expenditures for hunting, total	**488,380**	**240**	**2,038**	**2,027**
Trip-related expenditures	193,365	193	1,002	803
Hunting equipment.................................	111,695	185	604	464
Auxiliary equipment[1]................................	23,285	88	264	97
Special equipment[2].................................	...	...	...	...
Other[3]	91,946	167	552	382
Unspecified expenditures for fishing and hunting, total[4]	**154,027**	**99**	**1,560**	**237**
OUT OF STATE				
Expenditures for fishing and hunting, total	**178,372**	**126**	**1,421**	**1,465**
Trip-related expenditures	110,654	104	1,063	909
Equipment (fishing and hunting)........................	*25,400	*40	*628	*209
Auxiliary equipment[1]................................	...	...	...	...
Special equipment[2].................................	...	...	...	...
Other[3]	30,805	86	360	253
Expenditures for fishing, total	**49,920**	**63**	**796**	**783**
Trip-related expenditures	*30,157	*41	*731	*473
Fishing equipment	...	...	...	...
Auxiliary equipment[1]................................	...	...	...	...
Special equipment[2].................................	...	...	...	...
Other[3]	*1,042	*21	*49	*16
Expenditures for hunting, total	**127,810**	**76**	**1,675**	**1,702**
Trip-related expenditures	80,497	72	1,112	1,072
Hunting equipment.................................	...	...	...	...
Auxiliary equipment[1]................................	...	...	...	...
Special equipment[2].................................	...	...	...	...
Other[3]	*29,198	*57	*516	*389
Unspecified expenditures for fishing and hunting, total[4]	...	...	...	...

* Estimate based on a sample size of 10–29.   ... Sample size too small to report data reliably.

[1] Includes tents, special hunting or fishing clothing, etc.
[2] Includes boats, campers, 4x4 vehicles, cabins, etc.
[3] Includes magazines, books, membership dues, contributions, land leasing and ownership, stamps, tags, and licenses.
[4] Respondent could not specify whether expenditure was primarily for either fishing or hunting.

Note: Detail does not add to total because of multiple responses and nonresponse.

Table 24. Wildlife Watching in Louisiana by State Residents and Nonresidents Combined: 2006

(Population 16 years old and older. Numbers in thousands)

Participants	Number	Percent
Total participants	**738**	**100**
Away from home	*225	*30
Observe wildlife	*200	*27
Photograph wildlife	*82	*11
Feed wildlife	*116	*16
Around the home	671	91
Observe wildlife	491	66
Photograph wildlife	*125	*17
Feed wildlife	598	81
Visit public parks[1]	...	...
Maintain plantings or natural areas	*192	*26

* Estimate based on a sample size of 10–29.   ... Sample size too small to report data reliably.

[1] Includes visits only to parks or publicly owned areas within 1 mile of home.

Note: Detail does not add to total because of multiple responses.

Table 25. Participants, Trips, and Days of Participation in Away-From-Home Wildlife Watching in Louisiana: 2006

(Population 16 years old and older. Numbers in thousands)

Participants, trips, and days of participation	Activity in Louisiana					
	Total, state residents and nonresidents		State residents		Nonresidents	
	Number	Percent	Number	Percent	Number	Percent
PARTICIPANTS						
Total participants	*225	*100	*193	*100	...	...
Observe wildlife	*200	*89	*168	*87	...	...
Photograph wildlife	*82	*36	...	...	...	...
Feed wildlife	*116	*51	*106	*55	...	...
TRIPS						
Total trips	*979	*100	*902	*100	...	...
Average days per trip	*3	(X)	*3	(X)	...	(X)
DAYS						
Total days	*3,199	*100	*3,076	*100	...	...
Observing wildlife	*1,639	*51	*1,517	*49	...	...
Photographing wildlife	*814	*25	...	...	...	...
Feeding wildlife	*1,142	*36	...	...	...	...
Average days per participant	*14	(X)	*16	(X)	...	(X)
Observing wildlife	*8	(X)	*9	(X)	...	(X)
Photographing wildlife	*10	(X)	...	(X)	...	(X)
Feeding wildlife	*10	(X)	...	(X)	...	(X)

* Estimate based on a sample size of 10–29.   ... Sample size too small to report data reliably.   (X) Not applicable.

Note: Detail does not add to total because of multiple responses and nonresponse.

Table 26. Away-From-Home Wildlife-Watching Participants by Wildlife Observed, Photographed, or Fed in Louisiana: 2006

(Population 16 years old and older. Numbers in thousands)

Wildlife observed, photographed, or fed	Total, state residents and nonresidents		State residents		Nonresidents	
	Number	Percent	Number	Percent	Number	Percent
Total all wildlife	*225	*100	*193	*86	...	...
Total birds..	*197	*100	*165	*84	...	...
Songbirds (cardinals, robins, warblers, etc.)..........	*125	*100	*105	*84	...	...
Birds of prey (hawks, owls, eagles, etc.)	...	...	...	...	...	...
Waterfowl (ducks, geese, swan, etc.)	*169	*100	*142	*84	...	...
Other water birds (shorebirds, herons, cranes, etc.)....	*127	*100	*102	*80	...	...
Other birds (pheasants, turkeys, road runners, etc.)....	...	...	...	...	...	...
Total land mammals	*150	*100	*132	*88	...	...
Large land mammals (bears, bison, etc.)	*100	*100	...	...	...	...
Small land mammals (prairie dogs, squirrels, etc.)	*89	*100	...	...	...	...
Fish (salmon, shark, etc.)...........................	*89	*100	...	...	...	...
Marine mammals (whales, dolphins, etc.)	...	...	...	...	...	...
Other wildlife (butterflies, turtles, etc.)...............	*113	*100	*97	*86	...	...

* Estimate based on a sample size of 10–29.   ... Sample size too small to report data reliably.

Note: Detail does not add to total because of multiple responses.

Table 27. Participation in Wildlife-Watching Activities Around the Home in Louisiana: 2006

(State population 16 years old and older. Numbers in thousands)

Around the home	Participants		Around the home	Participants	
	Number	Percent		Number	Percent
Total around-the-home participants...	**671**	**100**	11 to 50 days	...	...
Observe wildlife...................	491	73	51 to 200 days	*202	*41
Visit public parks[1]	...	...	201 days or more	*140	*29
Photograph wildlife	*125	*19	**Participants Visiting Public Parks** [1]		
Feed wildlife......................	598	89	**Total, 1 day or more ....**	...	...
Maintain natural areas	*162	*24	1 to 5 days.....................	...	...
Maintain plantings	*155	*23	6 to 10 days	...	...
Participants Observing Wildlife			11 days or more	...	...
Total, all wildlife.................	**491**	**100**	**Participants Photographing Wildlife**		
Birds..........................	467	95	**Total, 1 day or more ....**	***125**	***100**
Land mammals..................	412	84	1 to 3 days.....................	...	...
Large mammals	*139	*28	4 to 10 days	...	...
Small mammals	412	84	11 or more days	...	...
Amphibians or reptiles	*178	*36	**Participants Feeding Wildlife**		
Insects or spiders	*135	*27	**Total, all wildlife.................**	**598**	**100**
Fish and other wildlife	*119	*24	Wild birds	578	97
			Other wildlife	260	44
Total, 1 day or more	**491**	**100**			
1 to 10 days	...	...			

* Estimate based on a sample size of 10–29.   ... Sample size too small to report data reliably.

[1] Includes visits only to parks or publicly owned areas within 1 mile of home.

Note: Detail does not add to total because of multiple responses and nonresponse.

Table 28. Louisiana Residents Participating in Wildlife Watching in the United States: 2006

(State population 16 years old and older. Numbers in thousands)

Participants	Number	Percent of participants	Percent of population
Total participants	**712**	**100**	**21**
Away from home	*234	*33	*7
Around the home	671	94	20
Observe wildlife.....................................	491	69	14
Photograph wildlife..................................	*125	*18	*4
Feed wild birds or other wildlife.........................	598	84	17
Maintain plantings or natural areas............................	*192	*27	*6
Visit public parks....................................	...	...	...

* Estimate based on a sample size of 10–29.   ... Sample size too small to report data reliably.

Note: Detail does not add to total because of multiple responses. The column showing percent of participants is based on total participants. The column showing percent of population is based on the state population 16 years old and older, including those who did not participate in wildlife watching.

Table 29. **Wild Bird Observers and Days of Observation in Louisiana by State Residents and Nonresidents: 2006**

(Population 16 years old and older. Numbers in thousands)

Observers and days of observation	Total, state residents and nonresidents		State residents		Nonresidents	
	Number	Percent	Number	Percent	Number	Percent
OBSERVERS						
Total bird observers......................	**552**	**100**	**520**	**100**	...	...
Around-the-home observers................	467	85	467	90	...	...
Away-from-home observers................	*197	*36	*165	*32	...	...
DAYS						
Total days observing birds	**68,283**	**100**	**68,160**	**100**	...	...
Around the home........................	65,471	96	65,471	96	...	...
Away from home........................	*2,811	*4	*2,689	*4	...	...

* Estimate based on a sample size of 10–29.   ... Sample size too small to report data reliably.

Note: Detail does not add to total because of multiple responses.

Table 30. Selected Characteristics of Louisiana Residents Participating in Wildlife Watching: 2006

(State population 16 years old and older. Numbers in thousands)

Characteristic	Population		Participants								
			Total			Away from home			Around the home		
	Number	Percent	Number	Percent who partici-pated	Percent	Number	Percent who partici-pated	Percent	Number	Percent who partici-pated	Percent
Total persons......................	3,433	100	712	21	100	*234	*7	*100	671	20	100
Population Density of Residence											
Urban	2,322	68	487	21	68	*137	*6	*59	446	19	66
Rural.......................	1,110	32	*225	*20	*32	...	...	...	*225	*20	*34
Population Size of Residence											
Metropolitan statistical area											
(MSA)......................	3,008	88	553	18	78	*180	*6	*77	512	17	76
1,000,000 or more	768	22	*169	*22	*24	...	...	...	*163	*21	*24
250,000 to 999,999	1,000	29	*145	*14	*20	...	...	...	*145	*14	*22
Less than 250,000	1,239	36	*239	*19	*34	*112	*9	*48	*204	*16	*30
Outside MSA	425	12	*159	*37	*22	...	...	...	*159	*37	*24
Sex											
Male........................	1,613	47	343	21	48	*104	*6	*45	323	20	48
Female	1,820	53	369	20	52	*129	*7	*55	349	19	52
Age											
16 to 17 years	126	4	...	...	...	...	...	...	...	...	...
18 to 24 years	347	10	...	...	...	...	...	...	...	...	...
25 to 34 years	526	15	...	...	...	...	...	...	...	...	...
35 to 44 years	599	17	*174	*29	*24	...	...	...	*157	*26	*23
45 to 54 years	647	19	*100	*15	*14	...	...	...	*100	*15	*15
55 to 64 years	547	16	*205	*37	*29	...	...	...	*205	*37	*30
65 years and older	642	19	*125	*19	*18	...	...	...	*115	*18	*17
Ethnicity											
Hispanic	77	2	...	...	...	...	...	...	...	...	...
Non-Hispanic	3,356	98	706	21	99	*234	*7	*100	665	20	99
Race											
White	2,343	68	590	25	83	*219	*9	*94	549	23	82
Black.......................	1,017	30	...	...	...	...	...	...	...	...	...
All others	73	2	...	...	...	...	...	...	...	...	...
Annual Household Income											
Under $10,000	329	10	...	...	...	...	...	...	...	...	...
$10,000 to $19,999	313	9	...	...	...	...	...	...	...	...	...
$20,000 to $29,999	329	10	...	...	...	...	...	...	...	...	...
$30,000 to $39,999	362	11	...	...	...	...	...	...	...	...	...
$40,000 to $49,999	256	7	*128	*50	*18	...	...	...	*128	*50	*19
$50,000 to $74,999	479	14	*96	*20	*13	...	...	...	*79	*16	*12
$75,000 to $99,999	317	9	...	...	...	...	...	...	...	...	...
$100,000 or more................	163	5	...	...	...	...	...	...	...	...	...
Not reported	885	26	...	...	...	...	...	...	...	...	...
Education											
11 years or less	666	19	*87	*13	*12	...	...	...	*87	*13	*13
12 years	1,338	39	*272	*20	*38	...	...	...	*255	*19	*38
1 to 3 years college..............	725	21	*157	*22	*22	...	...	...	*143	*20	*21
4 years college or more...........	703	20	*196	*28	*28	...	...	...	*186	*26	*28

* Estimate based on a sample size of 10–29.   ... Sample size too small to report data reliably.

Note: Detail does not add to total because of multiple responses and nonresponse. Percent who participated shows the percent of each row's population who participated in the activity named by the column (the percent of those living in urban areas who participated, etc.). Percent columns show the percent of each column's participants who are described by the row heading (the percent of those who participated who live in urban areas, etc.).

Table 31. Expenditures in Louisiana by State Residents and Nonresidents Combined for Wildlife Watching: 2006

(Population 16 years old and older)

Expenditure item	Expenditures (thousands of dollars)	Average per participant (dollars)	Spenders		
			Number (thousands)	Percent of wildlife-watching participants[1]	Average per spender (dollars)
Total, all items......................................	312,430	422	579	78	540
TRIP EXPENDITURES					
Total trip-related....................................	*61,822	*275	*169	*75	*366
Food and lodging	*41,818	*186	*158	*70	*265
Food..	*37,672	*167	*158	*70	*238
Lodging.......................................	...	...	...	...	...
Transportation	*18,772	*83	*150	*67	*125
Other trip costs[2]	...	...	...	...	...
EQUIPMENT AND OTHER EXPENDITURES					
Total	250,608	338	532	72	471
Wildlife-watching equipment, total....................	102,097	137	493	67	207
Binoculars, spotting scopes	...	...	...	...	...
Film and developing...............................	*13,869	*19	*73	*10	*190
Cameras, special lenses, video cameras, and other photographic equipment	...	...	...	...	...
Day packs, carrying cases, and special clothing	...	...	...	...	...
Bird food......................................	26,820	36	384	52	70
Food for other wildlife.............................	*12,098	*16	*224	*30	*54
Nest boxes, bird houses, bird feeders, and bird baths.......	*14,182	*18	*231	*31	*61
Other equipment (including field guides)	...	...	...	...	...
Auxiliary equipment[3]	...	...	...	...	...
Special equipment[4]	...	...	...	...	...
Magazines and books	*5,873	*8	*113	*15	*52
Membership dues and contributions......................	...	...	...	...	...
Land leasing and ownership...........................	...	...	...	...	...
Plantings	*32,791	*44	*121	*16	*272

* Estimate based on a sample size of 10–29.   ... Sample size too small to report data reliably.

[1] Percent of wildlife-watching participants column for trip-related expenditures is based on away-from-home participants. For equipment and other expenditures, the percent of wildlife-watching participants column is based on total wildlife-watching participants.
[2] Includes equipment rental and fees for guides, pack trips, public land use and private land use, boat fuel, other boating costs, and heating and cooking fuel.
[3] Includes tents, tarps, frame packs and other backpacking equipment, other camping equipment, and other auxiliary equipment.
[4] Includes travel or tent trailers, off-the-road vehicles, pickups, campers or vans, motor homes, boats, and other special equipment.

Note: Detail does not add to total because of multiple responses and nonresponse.

Table 32. Trip and Equipment Expenditures in Louisiana for Wildlife Watching by Louisiana Residents and Nonresidents: 2006

(Population 16 years old and older)

Expenditure item	Amount (thousands of dollars)	Spenders (thousands)	Average per spender (dollars)	Average per participant (dollars)
STATE RESIDENTS AND NONRESIDENTS				
Total...	**250,231**	**564**	**444**	**337**
Food and lodging....................................	*41,818	*158	*265	*186
Transportation.......................................	*18,772	*150	*125	*83
Other trip costs[1]....................................	...	...	...	...
Equipment[2]...	188,409	507	372	253
STATE RESIDENTS				
Total...	**213,946**	**519**	**413**	**303**
Food and lodging....................................	*13,634	*133	*102	*71
Transportation.......................................	*12,240	*138	*89	*63
Other trip costs[1]....................................	...	...	...	...
Equipment[2]...	187,087	487	385	265
NONRESIDENTS				
Total...	...	...	...	...
Food and lodging....................................	...	...	...	...
Transportation.......................................	...	...	...	...
Other trip costs[1]....................................	...	...	...	...
Equipment[2]...	...	...	...	...

* Estimate based on a sample size of 10–29.　　　... Sample size too small to report data reliably.

[1] Includes equipment rental and fees for guides, pack trips, public land use, private land use, boat fuel, other boating costs, and heating and cooking fuel.
[2] Includes wildlife watching, auxiliary, and special equipment.

Note: Detail does not add to total because of multiple responses and nonresponse. See Table 33 for a detailed listing of expenditure items.

Table 33. **Wildlife-Watching Expenditures Both Inside and Outside Louisiana by Louisiana Residents: 2006**

(State population 16 years old and older)

| Expenditure item | Expenditures (thousands of dollars) | Average per participant (dollars) | Spenders | | |
			Number (thousands)	Percent of wildlife-watching participants[1]	Average per spender (dollars)
Total, all items.....................................	420,881	591	534	75	789
TRIP EXPENDITURES					
Total trip-related.................................	*118,317	*506	*168	*72	*705
Food and lodging	*75,654	*324	*157	*67	*483
Food..	*31,473	*135	*157	*67	*201
Lodging.......................................	...	...	...	...	...
Transportation	*40,242	*172	*155	*66	*259
Other trip costs[2]	...	...	...	...	...
EQUIPMENT AND OTHER EXPENDITURES					
Total	302,564	425	511	72	592
Wildlife-watching equipment, total....................	151,959	213	482	68	315
Binoculars, spotting scopes	*16,024	*23	*88	*12	*182
Film and developing..............................	*13,843	*19	*72	*10	*193
Cameras, special lenses, videocameras, and other photographic equipment	...	...	...	...	...
Day packs, carrying cases, and special clothing	...	...	...	...	...
Bird food.......................................	26,820	38	384	54	70
Food for other wildlife............................	*12,098	*17	*224	*31	*54
Nest boxes, bird houses, bird feeders, and bird baths.......	*12,939	*18	*212	*30	*61
Other equipment	...	...	...	...	...
Auxiliary equipment[3]	...	...	...	...	...
Special equipment[4]	...	...	...	...	...
Magazines and books	*5,873	*8	*113	*16	*52
Membership dues and contributions......................	...	...	...	...	...
Land leasing and ownership..........................	...	...	...	...	...
Plantings	*32,791	*46	*121	*17	*272

* Estimate based on a sample size of 10–29.   ... Sample size too small to report data reliably.

[1] Percent of wildlife-watching participants column for trip-related expenditures is based on away-from-home participants. For equipment and other expenditures, the percent of wildlife-watching participants column is based on total wildlife-watching participants.
[2] Includes equipment rental and fees for guides, pack trips, public land use and private land use, boat fuel, other boating costs, and heating and cooking fuel.
[3] Includes tents, tarps, frame packs and other backpacking equipment, other camping equipment, and other auxiliary equipment.
[4] Includes travel or tent trailers, off-the-road vehicles, pickups, campers or vans, motor homes, boats, and other special equipment.

Note: Detail does not add to total because of multiple responses and nonresponse.

Table 34. In-State and Out-of-State Expenditures by Louisiana Residents for Wildlife Watching: 2006

(State population 16 years old and older)

Expenditure item	Amount (thousands of dollars)	Spenders (thousands)	Average per spender (dollars)	Average per participant (dollars)
IN LOUISIANA				
Expenditures for wildlife watching, total	**276,145**	**534**	**517**	**391**
Trip-related expenditures.............................	*26,859	*144	*186	*139
Wildlife-watching equipment...........................	100,775	472	213	143
Auxiliary equipment	...	...	...	...
Special equipment	...	...	...	...
Other...	*62,199	*212	*293	*88
OUT OF STATE				
Expenditures for wildlife watching, total	...	...	...	...
Trip-related expenditures.............................	...	...	...	...
Wildlife-watching equipment...........................	...	...	...	...
Auxiliary equipment	...	...	...	...
Special equipment	...	...	...	...
Other...	...	...	...	...

* Estimate based on a sample size of 10–29.   ... Sample size too small to report data reliably.

Note: See Table 33 for detailed listing of expenditure items.

Table 35. Participation of Louisiana Resident Wildlife-Watching Participants in Fishing and Hunting: 2006

(State population 16 years old and older. Numbers in thousands)

Participants	Total wildlife watchers		Wildlife-watching activity			
			Away from home		Around the home	
	Number	Percent	Number	Percent	Number	Percent
Total participants.........................	**712**	**100**	***234**	***100**	**671**	**100**
Wildlife-watching participants who:						
Did not fish or hunt.......................	428	60	*115	*49	408	61
Fished or hunted	284	40	118	51	263	39
Fished.................................	253	36	105	45	236	35
Hunted	116	16	*54	*23	108	16

* Estimate based on a sample size of 10–29.

Note: Detail does not add to total because of multiple responses and nonresponse.

Table 36. Participation of Louisiana Resident Sportspersons in Wildlife-Watching Activities: 2006

(State population 16 years old and older. Numbers in thousands)

Sportspersons	Sportspersons		Anglers		Hunters	
	Number	Percent	Number	Percent	Number	Percent
Total sportspersons.............................	**678**	**100**	**598**	**100**	**275**	**100**
Sportspersons who:						
Did not engage in wildlife-watching activities	394	58	345	58	160	58
Engaged in wildlife-watching activities............	284	42	253	42	116	42
Away from home	118	17	105	18	*54	*20
Around the home	263	39	236	39	108	39

* Estimate based on a sample size of 10–29.

Note: Detail does not add to total because of multiple responses and nonresponse.

Table 37. Participation in Wildlife-Associated Recreation by State Residents Both Inside and Outside Their Resident State: 2006

(Population 16 years old and older. Numbers in thousands)

Participant's state of residence	Population	Total participants		Sportspersons		Wildlife-watching participants	
		Number	Percent of population	Number	Percent of population	Number	Percent of population
United States, total...........	229,245	87,465	38	33,916	15	71,132	31
Alabama......................	3,550	1,417	40	707	20	1,006	28
Alaska........................	499	288	58	149	30	207	42
Arizona.......................	4,585	1,233	27	418	9	988	22
Arkansas......................	2,156	1,082	50	551	26	859	40
California	27,299	6,804	25	1,783	7	5,799	21
Colorado......................	3,605	1,735	48	593	16	1,459	40
Connecticut...................	2,735	1,223	45	297	11	1,102	40
Delaware......................	669	256	38	85	13	212	32
Florida	14,233	4,626	33	2,004	14	3,520	25
Georgia.......................	6,910	2,415	35	1,161	17	1,819	26
Hawaii	1,014	227	22	100	10	160	16
Idaho.........................	1,102	564	51	259	24	432	39
Illinois........................	9,767	2,886	30	1,109	11	2,355	24
Indiana	4,799	2,279	47	822	17	1,825	38
Iowa	2,339	1,306	56	518	22	1,111	48
Kansas	2,110	979	46	425	20	787	37
Kentucky	3,260	1,667	51	670	21	1,341	41
Louisiana	3,433	1,106	32	678	20	712	21
Maine	1,074	717	67	266	25	600	56
Maryland	4,333	1,549	36	521	12	1,334	31
Massachusetts.................	5,032	1,931	38	472	9	1,725	34
Michigan......................	7,804	3,651	47	1,371	18	2,947	38
Minnesota.....................	4,021	2,480	62	1,280	32	1,946	48
Mississippi	2,214	896	40	537	24	618	28
Missouri	4,521	2,496	55	1,096	24	2,059	46
Montana	753	510	68	232	31	412	55
Nebraska......................	1,359	552	41	234	17	438	32
Nevada	1,895	530	28	182	10	420	22
New Hampshire	1,044	527	51	141	14	471	45
New Jersey....................	6,734	1,826	27	562	8	1,537	23
New Mexico...................	1,500	601	40	224	15	490	33
New York.....................	14,990	4,103	27	1,236	8	3,548	24
North Carolina	6,719	2,816	42	1,038	15	2,267	34
North Dakota	507	232	46	145	29	134	26
Ohio	8,889	4,022	45	1,488	17	3,379	38
Oklahoma.....................	2,743	1,372	50	602	22	1,082	39
Oregon	2,889	1,531	53	550	19	1,266	44
Pennsylvania..................	9,793	4,165	43	1,415	14	3,638	37
Rhode Island	842	355	42	86	10	312	37
South Carolina	3,315	1,283	39	595	18	943	28
South Dakota	601	327	54	136	23	266	44
Tennessee	4,699	2,287	49	775	16	1,966	42
Texas.........................	17,076	5,481	32	2,668	16	4,111	24
Utah	1,808	764	42	351	19	574	32
Vermont	506	311	62	91	18	279	55
Virginia.......................	5,893	2,500	42	857	15	2,126	36
Washington....................	4,980	2,315	46	764	15	2,007	40
West Virginia	1,458	735	50	364	25	585	40
Wisconsin.....................	4,350	2,217	51	1,185	27	1,710	39
Wyoming	405	229	57	113	28	194	48

Note: Detail does not add to total because of multiple responses. U.S. totals include responses from participants residing in the District of Columbia, as described in Appendix D.

Table 38. Anglers and Hunters by Sportsperson's State of Residence: 2006

(Population 16 years old and older. Numbers in thousands)

Sportsperson's state of residence	Population	Fished or hunted		Fished only		Hunted only		Fished and hunted	
		Number	Percent of population	Number	Percent of population	Number	Percent of population	Number	Percent of population
United States, total.....	**229,245**	**33,916**	**15**	**21,406**	**9**	**3,964**	**2**	**8,546**	**4**
Alabama	3,550	707	20	395	11	79	2	233	7
Alaska.	499	149	30	94	19	*11	*2	44	9
Arizona.	4,585	418	9	290	6	48	1	81	2
Arkansas.	2,156	551	26	244	11	88	4	220	10
California	27,299	1,783	7	1,465	5	*94	*(Z)	223	1
Colorado	3,605	593	16	460	13	*39	*1	94	3
Connecticut.	2,735	297	11	257	9	...	...	34	1
Delaware.	669	85	13	64	10	*9	*1	12	2
Florida	14,233	2,004	14	1,678	12	*54	*(Z)	271	2
Georgia.	6,910	1,161	17	805	12	*101	*1	255	4
Hawaii	1,014	100	10	81	8	...	...	*14	*1
Idaho.	1,102	259	24	136	12	*36	*3	88	8
Illinois.	9,767	1,109	11	837	9	*74	*1	198	2
Indiana	4,799	822	17	569	12	83	2	171	4
Iowa	2,339	518	22	308	13	70	3	141	6
Kansas	2,110	425	20	233	11	56	3	136	6
Kentucky	3,260	670	21	410	13	*49	*1	212	7
Louisiana	3,433	678	20	403	12	*81	*2	195	6
Maine	1,074	266	25	120	11	40	4	106	10
Maryland	4,333	521	12	370	9	46	1	105	2
Massachusetts.	5,032	472	9	406	8	*20	*(Z)	46	1
Michigan.	7,804	1,371	18	650	8	272	3	449	6
Minnesota.	4,021	1,280	32	745	19	*138	*3	398	10
Mississippi	2,214	537	24	293	13	*58	*3	186	8
Missouri	4,521	1,096	24	536	12	165	4	394	9
Montana	753	232	31	86	11	53	7	92	12
Nebraska.	1,359	234	17	129	10	42	3	63	5
Nevada	1,895	182	10	122	6	26	1	34	2
New Hampshire	1,044	141	14	89	9	*17	*2	35	3
New Jersey.	6,734	562	8	478	7	*32	*(Z)	53	1
New Mexico.	1,500	224	15	152	10	34	2	38	3
New York	14,990	1,236	8	734	5	207	1	295	2
North Carolina	6,719	1,038	15	734	11	*74	*1	230	3
North Dakota	507	145	29	59	12	40	8	47	9
Ohio	8,889	1,488	17	1,011	11	195	2	282	3
Oklahoma.	2,743	602	22	370	13	*55	*2	177	6
Oregon	2,889	550	19	331	11	67	2	152	5
Pennsylvania.	9,793	1,415	14	482	5	425	4	508	5
Rhode Island	842	86	10	73	9	...	...	*10	*1
South Carolina	3,315	595	18	429	13	*48	*1	119	4
South Dakota	601	136	23	46	8	41	7	50	8
Tennessee	4,699	775	16	491	10	*67	*1	217	5
Texas.	17,076	2,668	16	1,672	10	324	2	672	4
Utah	1,808	351	19	197	11	38	2	116	6
Vermont	506	91	18	34	7	20	4	37	7
Virginia.	5,893	857	15	497	8	127	2	233	4
Washington.	4,980	764	15	577	12	74	1	113	2
West Virginia	1,458	364	25	165	11	58	4	141	10
Wisconsin	4,350	1,185	27	534	12	160	4	492	11
Wyoming	405	113	28	61	15	*15	*4	37	9

* Estimate based on a sample size of 10–29.   ... Sample size too small to report data reliably.   (Z) Less than 0.5 percent.

Notes: U.S. totals include responses from participants residing in the District of Columbia, as described in Appendix D.

Table includes state residents' participation both inside and outside their resident state.

Table 39. **Participation in Wildlife-Associated Recreation in Each State by Both Residents and Nonresidents of the State: 2006**

(Population 16 years old and older. Numbers in thousands)

State where activity took place	Total participants		Sportspersons		Wildlife-watching participants	
	Number	Percent	Number	Percent	Number	Percent
United States, total...........	87,465	100	33,916	39	71,132	81
Alabama.................	1,719	100	962	56	1,161	68
Alaska.................	691	100	315	46	496	72
Arizona.................	1,546	100	493	32	1,277	83
Arkansas.................	1,419	100	790	56	1,011	71
California	7,385	100	1,814	25	6,270	85
Colorado.................	2,234	100	813	36	1,819	81
Connecticut.................	1,332	100	309	23	1,170	88
Delaware.................	395	100	189	48	285	72
Florida	5,886	100	2,815	48	4,240	72
Georgia.................	2,773	100	1,308	47	1,987	72
Hawaii	366	100	162	44	262	72
Idaho.................	1,005	100	440	44	754	75
Illinois.................	3,126	100	1,004	32	2,566	82
Indiana	2,610	100	886	34	2,042	78
Iowa	1,455	100	552	38	1,205	83
Kansas	1,107	100	544	49	816	74
Kentucky	1,906	100	820	43	1,475	77
Louisiana	1,221	100	769	63	738	60
Maine	1,007	100	411	41	801	80
Maryland	1,867	100	707	38	1,491	80
Massachusetts.................	2,205	100	532	24	1,919	87
Michigan.................	4,217	100	1,685	40	3,227	77
Minnesota.................	2,970	100	1,571	53	2,093	70
Mississippi	1,138	100	656	58	731	64
Missouri	2,876	100	1,300	45	2,248	78
Montana	950	100	378	40	755	79
Nebraska.................	650	100	259	40	490	75
Nevada	788	100	177	22	686	87
New Hampshire	839	100	258	31	710	85
New Jersey.................	2,100	100	696	33	1,713	82
New Mexico.................	947	100	316	33	787	83
New York.................	4,595	100	1,428	31	3,852	84
North Carolina	3,412	100	1,361	40	2,641	77
North Dakota	279	100	190	68	148	53
Ohio	4,247	100	1,488	35	3,489	82
Oklahoma.................	1,472	100	684	46	1,110	75
Oregon	1,837	100	661	36	1,484	81
Pennsylvania.................	4,663	100	1,520	33	3,947	85
Rhode Island	527	100	163	31	436	83
South Carolina	1,653	100	893	54	1,115	67
South Dakota	572	100	251	44	432	75
Tennessee	2,824	100	969	34	2,362	84
Texas.................	6,029	100	2,940	49	4,225	70
Utah	1,132	100	437	39	877	77
Vermont	545	100	150	27	468	86
Virginia.................	2,866	100	1,045	36	2,312	81
Washington.................	2,739	100	818	30	2,331	85
West Virginia	994	100	488	49	743	75
Wisconsin.................	2,913	100	1,582	54	2,039	70
Wyoming	762	100	264	35	643	84

Note: Detail does not add to total because of multiple responses. U.S. totals include responses from participants residing in the District of Columbia, as described in Appendix D.

Table 40. Anglers and Hunters by State Where Fishing or Hunting Took Place: 2006

(Population 16 years old and older. Numbers in thousands)

State where fishing or hunting took place	Anglers						Hunters					
	Total anglers, residents and nonresidents		Residents		Nonresidents		Total hunters, residents and nonresidents		Residents		Nonresidents	
	Number	Percent	Number	Percent	Number	Percent	Number	Percent	Number	Percent	Number	Percent
United States, total.....	29,952	100	27,641	92	6,494	22	12,510	100	11,971	96	1,826	15
Alabama...............	806	100	600	74	206	26	391	100	310	79	81	21
Alaska................	293	100	137	47	156	53	71	100	53	75	...	...
Arizona...............	422	100	330	78	92	22	159	100	126	79	*33	*21
Arkansas..............	655	100	430	66	225	34	354	100	301	85	*53	*15
California.............	1,730	100	1,578	91	152	9	281	100	274	97	...	...
Colorado..............	660	100	490	74	171	26	259	100	126	49	134	51
Connecticut............	302	100	251	83	51	17	38	100	36	96	...	...
Delaware..............	159	100	66	41	*94	*59	42	100	19	46	...	...
Florida	2,767	100	1,881	68	885	32	236	100	214	91	*22	*9
Georgia...............	1,107	100	971	88	136	12	481	100	344	72	136	28
Hawaii	157	100	92	58	*65	*42	18	100	18	98	...	...
Idaho.................	350	100	206	59	144	41	187	100	122	65	65	35
Illinois................	873	100	795	91	78	9	316	100	258	82	*58	*18
Indiana	768	100	663	86	106	14	272	100	237	87	*35	*13
Iowa	438	100	397	91	*40	*9	251	100	208	83	*44	*17
Kansas	404	100	319	79	85	21	271	100	183	68	88	32
Kentucky	721	100	580	80	141	20	291	100	241	83	*50	*17
Louisiana	702	100	590	84	112	16	270	100	241	89	...	...
Maine	351	100	220	63	131	37	175	100	146	83	*29	*17
Maryland	645	100	403	62	242	38	161	100	133	83	*28	*17
Massachusetts..........	497	100	398	80	99	20	73	100	57	79	*16	*21
Michigan..............	1,394	100	1,077	77	318	23	753	100	721	96	*32	*4
Minnesota.............	1,427	100	1,108	78	319	22	535	100	509	95	*26	*5
Mississippi	546	100	465	85	80	15	304	100	238	78	*66	*22
Missouri	1,076	100	871	81	206	19	608	100	540	89	69	11
Montana	291	100	172	59	119	41	197	100	145	74	*52	*26
Nebraska..............	198	100	169	85	*29	*15	118	100	102	86	...	...
Nevada	142	100	114	81	*27	*19	63	100	54	85	...	...
New Hampshire	230	100	108	47	122	53	61	100	51	85	*9	*15
New Jersey............	654	100	458	70	197	30	89	100	72	81	...	...
New Mexico...........	248	100	164	66	*84	*34	99	100	66	67	*32	*33
New York.............	1,153	100	932	81	221	19	566	100	491	87	75	13
North Carolina	1,263	100	868	69	395	31	304	100	277	91	*27	*9
North Dakota	106	100	88	84	...	...	128	100	86	67	*42	*33
Ohio	1,256	100	1,145	91	112	9	500	100	467	93	...	...
Oklahoma.............	611	100	525	86	86	14	251	100	224	89	*27	*11
Oregon	576	100	455	79	122	21	237	100	218	92	...	...
Pennsylvania...........	994	100	830	83	164	17	1,044	100	933	89	111	11
Rhode Island	158	100	76	48	82	52	14	100	12	84	...	...
South Carolina	810	100	527	65	283	35	208	100	159	77	*49	*23
South Dakota	135	100	89	66	45	34	171	100	89	52	81	48
Tennessee	871	100	658	75	214	25	329	100	265	81	*64	*19
Texas.................	2,527	100	2,308	91	218	9	1,101	100	979	89	123	11
Utah	375	100	288	77	87	23	166	100	144	86	*23	*14
Vermont	114	100	64	56	50	44	73	100	56	76	*17	*24
Virginia...............	858	100	640	75	218	25	413	100	353	86	*60	*14
Washington............	736	100	641	87	95	13	182	100	179	98	...	...
West Virginia	376	100	291	77	86	23	269	100	194	72	*75	*28
Wisconsin.............	1,394	100	1,014	73	381	27	697	100	649	93	*48	*7
Wyoming	203	100	96	47	107	53	102	100	50	49	52	51

* Estimate based on a sample size of 10–29.   ... Sample size too small to report data reliably.

Note: Detail does not add to total because of multiple responses. U.S. totals include responses from participants residing in the District of Columbia, as described in Appendix D.

Appendix A

Appendix A.
Definitions

Annual household income—Total 2006 income of household members before taxes and other deductions.

Around-the-home wildlife watching—Activity within 1 mile of home with one of six primary purposes: (1) taking special interest in or trying to identify birds or other wildlife; (2) photographing wildlife; (3) feeding birds or other wildlife; (4) maintaining natural areas of at least 1/4 acre for the benefit of wildlife; (5) maintaining plantings (such as shrubs and agricultural crops) for the benefit of wildlife; and (6) visiting public land to observe, photograph, or feed wildlife.

Auxiliary equipment—Equipment owned primarily for wildlife-associated recreation. For the sportspersons section, these include sleeping bags, packs, duffel bags, tents, binoculars and field glasses, special fishing and hunting clothing, foul weather gear, boots and waders, maintenance and repair of equipment, and processing and taxidermy costs. For the wildlife-watching section, these include tents, tarps, frame packs, backpacking and other camping equipment, and blinds.

Away-from-home wildlife watching—Trips or outings at least 1 mile from home for the primary purpose of observing, photographing, or feeding wildlife. Trips to zoos, circuses, aquariums, and museums are not included.

Big game—Bear, deer, elk, moose, wild turkey, and similar large animals that are hunted.

Census Divisions

East North Central
Illinois
Indiana
Michigan
Ohio
Wisconsin

East South Central
Alabama
Kentucky
Mississippi
Tennessee

Middle Atlantic
New Jersey
New York
Pennsylvania

Mountain
Arizona
Colorado
Idaho
Montana
Nevada
New Mexico
Utah
Wyoming

New England
Connecticut
Maine
Massachusetts
New Hampshire
Rhode Island
Vermont

Pacific
Alaska
California
Hawaii
Oregon
Washington

South Atlantic
Delaware
District of Columbia
Florida
Georgia
Maryland
North Carolina
South Carolina
Virginia
West Virginia

West North Central
Kansas
Iowa
Minnesota

Missouri
Nebraska
North Dakota
South Dakota

West South Central
Arkansas
Louisiana
Oklahoma
Texas

Day—Any part of a day spent participating in a given activity. For example, if someone hunted two hours one day and three hours another day, it would be reported as two days of hunting. If someone hunted two hours in the morning and three hours in the afternoon of the same day, it would be considered one day of hunting.

Education—The highest completed grade of school or year of college.

Expenditures—Money spent in 2006 for wildlife-related recreation trips in the United States, wildlife-related recreational equipment purchased in the United States, and other items. The "other items" were books and magazines, membership dues and contributions, land leasing or owning, hunting and fishing licenses, and plantings, all for the purpose of wildlife-related recreation. Expenditures included both money spent by participants for themselves and the value of gifts they received.

Fishing—The sport of catching or attempting to catch fish with a hook and line, bow and arrow, or spear; it also includes catching or gathering shellfish (clams, crabs, etc.); and the noncommercial seining or netting of fish, unless the fish are for use as bait. For example, seining for smelt is fishing, but seining for bait minnows is not included as fishing.

Fishing equipment—Items owned primarily for fishing:

Rods, reels, poles, and rod-making components

Lines and leaders

Artificial lures, flies, baits, and dressing for flies or lines

Hooks, sinkers, swivels, and other items attached to a line, except lures and baits

Tackle boxes

Creels, stringers, fish bags, landing nets, and gaff hooks

Minnow traps, seines, and bait containers

Depth finders, fish finders, and other electronic fishing devices

Ice fishing equipment

Other fishing equipment

Freshwater—Reservoirs, lakes, ponds, and the nontidal portions of rivers and streams.

Great Lakes fishing—Fishing in Lakes Superior, Michigan, Huron, St. Clair, Erie, and Ontario, their connecting waters such as the St. Mary's River system, Detroit River, St. Clair River, and the Niagara River, and the St. Lawrence River south of the bridge at Cornwall, New York. Great Lakes fishing includes fishing in tributaries of the Great Lakes for smelt, steelhead, and salmon.

Home—The starting point of a wildlife-related recreational trip. It may be a permanent residence or a temporary or seasonal residence such as a cabin.

Hunting—The sport of shooting or attempting to shoot wildlife with firearms or archery equipment.

Hunting equipment—Items owned primarily for hunting:

Rifles, shotguns, muzzleloaders, and handguns

Archery equipment

Telescopic sights

Decoys and game calls

Ammunition

Hand-loading equipment

Hunting dogs and associated costs

Other hunting equipment

Land leasing and owning—Leasing or owning land either singly or in cooperation with others for the primary purpose of fishing, hunting, or wildlife watching on it.

Maintain natural areas—To set aside 1/4 acre or more of natural environment, such as wood lots or open fields, for the primary purpose of benefiting wildlife. This is categorized as a wildlife-watching activity, not fishing or hunting.

Maintain plantings—To introduce or encourage the growth of food and cover plants for the primary purpose of benefiting wildlife. Examples of plantings are butterfly bushes and various sumacs. This is categorized as a wildlife-watching activity, not fishing or hunting.

Metropolitan statistical area (MSA)—Except in the New England States, an MSA is a county or group of contiguous counties containing at least one city of 50,000 or more inhabitants or twin cities (i.e., cities with contiguous boundaries and constituting, for general social and economic purposes, a single community) with a combined population of at least 50,000. Also included in an MSA are contiguous counties that are socially and economically integrated with the central city. In the New England States, an MSA consists of towns and cities instead of counties. Each MSA must include at least one central city. See U.S. Census Bureau publication *State and Metropolitan Area Data Book; 2006* for more detailed information on MSAs. It can be found at <http://www.census.gov/prod/2006pubs/smadb/smadb-06.pdf>.

Migratory birds—Birds that regularly migrate from one region or climate to another such as ducks, geese, and doves and other birds that may be hunted.

Multiple responses—The term used to reflect the fact that individuals or their characteristics fall into more than one reporting category. An example of a big game hunter who hunted for deer and elk demonstrates the effect of multiple responses. In this case, adding the number of deer hunters (one) and elk hunters (one) would overstate the number of big game hunters (one)

because deer and elk hunters are not mutually exclusive categories. In contrast, total participants is the sum of male and female participants, because "male" and "female" are mutually exclusive categories.

Nonresidents—Individuals who do not live in the State being reported. For example, a person living in Texas who watches whales in California is a nonresidential wildlife-watcher in California.

Nonresponse—A term used to reflect the fact that some Survey respondents provide incomplete sets of information. For example, a Survey respondent may have been unable to identify the primary type of hunting for which a gun was bought. Total hunting expenditure estimates will include the gun purchase, but it will not appear as spending for big game or any other type of hunting. Nonresponses result in reported totals that are greater than the sum of their parts.

Observe—To take special interest in or try to identify birds, fish, or other wildlife.

Other animals—Coyotes, crows, foxes, groundhogs, prairie dogs, raccoons, and similar animals that can be legally hunted and are not classified as big game, small game, or migratory birds. They may be classified as unprotected or predatory animals by the State in which they are hunted. Feral pigs are classified as "other animals" in all States except Hawaii, where they are considered big game.

Participants—Individuals who engage in fishing, hunting, or a wildlife-watching activity. Unless otherwise stated, a person has to have hunted, fished, or wildlife watched in 2006 to be considered a participant.

Plantings—See "Maintain plantings."

Primary purpose—The principal motivation for an activity, trip, or expenditure.

Private land—Land that is owned by a private individual, group of individuals, or nongovernmental organization.

Public land—Land that is owned by local governments (such as county parks and municipal watersheds), State governments (such as State parks and wildlife management areas), or federal governments (such as National Forests and Wildlife Refuges).

Public parks or areas—See "Public land."

Residents—Individuals who lived in the State being reported. For example, a person who lives in California and watches whales in California is a residential wildlife watcher in California.

Rural—All territory, population, and housing units located outside of urbanized areas and urban clusters, as determined by the Census Bureau.

Saltwater—Oceans, tidal bays and sounds, and the tidal portions of rivers and streams.

Screening interviews—The first Survey contact with a sample household. Screening interviews are conducted with a household representative to identify respondents who are eligible for in-depth interviews. Screening interviews gather data such as age and sex about individuals in the households. Further information on screening interviews is available on page vii in the "Survey Background and Method" section of this report.

Small game—Grouse, pheasants, quail, rabbits, squirrels, and similar small animals for which States have small game seasons and bag limits.

Special equipment—Big-ticket equipment items that are owned primarily for wildlife-related recreation:

Bass boats

Other types of motorboats

Canoes and other types of non-motorboats

Boat motors, boat trailer/hitches, and other boat accessories

Pickups, campers, vans, travel or tent trailers, motor homes, house trailers, recreational vehicles (RVs)

Cabins

Off-the-road vehicles such as trail bikes, all terrain vehicles (ATVs), dune buggies, four-wheelers, 4x4 vehicles, and snowmobiles

Other special equipment

Spenders—People who spent money on fishing, hunting, or wildlife-watching activities or equipment.

Sportspersons—Individuals who engage in fishing, hunting, or both.

Trip—An outing involving fishing, hunting, or wildlife watching. A trip may begin from an individual's principal residence or from another place, such as a vacation home or the home of a relative. A trip may last an hour, a day, or many days.

Type of fishing—There are three types of fishing: (1) freshwater except Great Lakes, (2) Great Lakes, and (3) saltwater.

Type of hunting—There are four types of hunting: (1) big game, (2) small game, (3) migratory bird, and (4) other animal.

Unspecified expenditure—An item that was purchased for use in both fishing and hunting, rather than primarily one or the other. Auxiliary equipment, special equipment, magazines and books, and membership dues and contributions are the items for which a purchase could be categorized as "unspecified."

Urban—All territory, population, and housing units located within boundaries that encompass densely settled territory, consisting of core census block groups or blocks that have a population density of at least 1,000 people per square mile and surrounding census blocks that have an overall density of at least 500 people per square mile. Under certain conditions, less densely settled territory may be included, as determined by the Census Bureau.

Wildlife—Animals, such as birds, fish, insects, mammals, amphibians, and reptiles that are living in natural or wild environments. Wildlife does not include animals living in aquariums, zoos, and other artificial surroundings or domestic animals such as farm animals or pets.

Wildlife-associated recreation—Recreational fishing, hunting, and wildlife watching.

Wildlife watching—There are six types of wildlife watching: (1) closely observing, (2) photographing, (3) feeding, (4) visiting public parks or areas, (5) maintaining plantings, and (6) maintaining natural areas. These activities must be the primary purpose of the trip or the around-the-home undertaking.

Wildlife observed, photographed, or fed—Examples of species that wildlife watchers observe, photograph, and/or feed are (1) Wild birds—songbirds such as cardinals, robins, warblers, jays, buntings, and sparrows; birds of prey such as hawks, owls, eagles, and falcons; waterfowl such as ducks, geese, and swans; other water birds such as shorebirds, herons, pelicans, and cranes; and other birds such as pheasants, turkeys, road runners, and woodpeckers; (2) Land mammals—large land mammals such as bears, bison, deer, moose, and elk; and small land mammals such as squirrels, foxes, prairie dogs, and rabbits; (3) Fish such as salmon, sharks, and groupers; (4) Marine mammals such as whales, dolphins, and manatees; and (5) Other wildlife such as butterflies, turtles, spiders, and snakes.

Wildlife-watching equipment—Items owned primarily for observing, photographing, or feeding wildlife:

Binoculars and spotting scopes

Cameras, video cameras, special lenses, and other photographic equipment

Film and developing

Commercially prepared and packaged wild bird food

Other bulk food used to feed wild birds

Food for other wildlife

Nest boxes, bird houses, feeders, and baths

Day packs, carrying cases, and special clothing

Other items such as field guides and maps

Appendix B

Appendix B.
2005 Participation of 6- to 15-Year-Olds: Data From Screening Interviews

The *2006 National Survey of Fishing, Hunting, and Wildlife-Associated Recreation* was carried out in two phases. The first (or screening) phase began in April 2006. The main purpose of this phase was to collect information about all persons 16 years old and older in order to develop a sample of potential sportspersons and wildlife watchers for the second (or detailed) phase. Also, information was collected on the number of persons 6 to 15 years old who participated in wildlife-related recreation activities in 2005.

It is important to emphasize that the information reported from the 2006 screen relates to activity only up to and including 2005. Also, these data are reported in most cases by one household respondent speaking for all household members rather than the actual participant. In addition, these data are based on long-term recall (at least a 12-month recall), which has been found in Survey research (Investigation of Possible Recall/Reference Period Bias in National Surveys of Fishing, Hunting, and Wildlife-Associated Recreation, December 1989, Westat, Inc.) to add bias to the resulting estimates. In many cases, longer recall periods result in overestimating participation and expenditures for wildlife-related recreation.

Tables B-1 through B-4 report data on 6-to-15-year-old participants in 2005. Detailed expenditure and recreational activity data were not gathered for the 6-to-15-year-old participants.

Because of differences in methodologies of the screening and the detailed phases of the 2006 Survey, resulting estimates are not comparable. Only participants 16 years old and older were eligible for the detailed phase. The detailed phase was a series of three interviews conducted at four-month intervals. The screening interviews were one year or more recall. The shorter recall period of the detailed phase had better data accuracy.

Table B-1. **Louisiana Residents 6 to 15 Years Old Participating in Fishing and Hunting Both Inside and Outside Louisiana: 2005**

(State population 6 to 15 years old. Numbers in thousands)

Sportspersons	Sportspersons 6 to 15 years old		
	Number	Percent of sportspersons	Percent of population
Total sportspersons	167	100	27
Total anglers	163	98	26
Fished only...	120	72	19
Fished and hunted	*43	*26	*7
Total hunters..	*47	*28	*8
Hunted only...	...	...	...
Hunted and fished	*43	*26	*7

* Estimate based on a sample size of 10–29.   ... Sample size too small to report data reliably.

Note: Detail does not add to total because of multiple responses. Column showing percent of sportspersons is based on the "Total sportspersons" row. Column showing percent of population is based on the state population 6 to 15 years old, including those who did not fish or hunt. Data reported on this table are from screening interviews in which one adult household member responded for household members 6 to 15 years old. The screening interview required the respondent to recall 12 months' worth of activity. Includes state residents who fished or hunted only in other countries.

Table B-2. Selected Characteristics of Louisiana Resident Anglers and Hunters 6 to 15 Years Old: 2005

(State population 6 to 15 years old. Numbers in thousands)

Characteristic	Population		Sportspersons (fished or hunted)			Anglers			Hunters		
	Number	Percent	Number	Percent who partici-pated	Percent	Number	Percent who partici-pated	Percent	Number	Percent who partici-pated	Percent
Total persons	**620**	**100**	**167**	**27**	**100**	**163**	**26**	**100**	***47**	***8**	***100**
Population Density of Residence											
Urban..................	441	71	112	25	67	110	25	67	*28	*6	*59
Rural	180	29	*55	*31	*33	*53	*30	*33	...	...	...
Population Size of Residence											
Metropolitan statistical areas (MSA)................	534	86	142	27	85	140	26	86	*33	*6	*71
1,000,000 or more	144	23	...	...	...	...	...	...	...	...	...
250,000 to 999,999......	165	27	*54	*32	*32	*52	*31	*32	...	...	...
Less than 250,000.......	224	36	*71	*32	*43	*71	*32	*44	...	...	...
Outside MSA	87	14	*25	*29	*15	...	...	...	...	...	...
Sex											
Male	309	50	93	30	55	89	29	54	*33	*11	*71
Female.................	311	50	*74	*24	*45	*74	*24	*46	...	...	...
Age											
6 to 8 years.............	187	30	*29	*15	*17	*27	*14	*17	...	...	...
9 to 11 years............	231	37	*60	*26	*36	*60	*26	*37	...	...	...
12 to 15 years...........	202	33	*78	*39	*47	*76	*38	*47	*31	*15	*66
Ethnicity											
Hispanic	...	...	...	...	...	...	...	...	...	...	...
Non-Hispanic	616	99	163	26	98	159	26	98	*47	*8	*100
Race											
White..................	361	58	128	35	76	124	34	76	*45	*12	*96
Black..................	240	39	...	...	...	...	...	...	...	...	...
All others	...	...	...	...	...	...	...	...	...	...	...
Annual Household Income											
Less than $10,000........	*56	*9	...	...	...	...	...	...	...	...	...
$10,000 to $19,999........	...	...	...	...	...	...	...	...	...	...	...
$20,000 to $29,999........	95	15	...	...	...	...	...	...	...	...	...
$30,000 to $39,999........	86	14	*33	*38	*20	*33	*38	*20	...	...	...
$40,000 to $49,999........	*34	*6	...	...	...	...	...	...	...	...	...
$50,000 to $74,999........	137	22	*28	*21	*17	*28	*21	*17	...	...	...
$75,000 or more	109	18	*37	*34	*22	*37	*34	*23	...	...	...
Not reported	69	11	...	...	...	...	...	...	...	...	...

* Estimate based on a sample size of 10–29.   ... Sample size too small to report data reliably.

Note: Percent who participated shows the percent of each row's population who participated in the activity named by the column (the percent of those living in urban areas who fished, etc.). Remaining percent columns show the percent of each column's participants who are described by the row heading (the percent of anglers who lived in urban areas, etc.). Data reported on this table are from screening interviews in which one adult household member responded for household members 6 to 15 years old. The screening interview required the respondent to recall 12 months' worth of activity. Includes state residents who fished or hunted only in other countries.

Table B-3. Louisiana Residents 6 to 15 Years Old Participating in Wildlife Watching Both Inside and Outside Louisiana: 2005

(State population 6 to 15 years old. Numbers in thousands)

Participants	Number	Percent of participants	Percent of population
Total participants...	160	100	26
Away from home...	*74	*46	*12
Around the home..	143	89	23
Observe wildlife..	128	80	21
Photograph wildlife.......................................	...	...	...
Feed wild birds or other wildlife	96	60	15
Maintain plantings or natural areas...........................	*21	*13	*3

* Estimate based on a sample size of 10–29.   ... Sample size too small to report data reliably.

Note: Detail does not add to total because of multiple responses. The column showing percent of participants is based on total participants. The column showing percent of population is based on the state population 6 to 15 years old, including those who did not participate in wildlife watching. Data reported on this table are from screening interviews in which one adult household member responded for household members 6 to 15 years old. The screening interview required the respondent to recall 12 months' worth of activity. Includes state residents who wildlife watched only in other countries.

Table B-4. **Selected Characteristics of Louisiana Resident Wildlife Watchers 6 to 15 Years Old: 2005**

(State population 6 to 15 years old. Numbers in thousands)

Characteristic	Population		Total wildlife watchers			Away from home			Around the home		
	Number	Percent	Number	Percent who partici-pated	Percent	Number	Percent who partici-pated	Percent	Number	Percent who partici-pated	Percent
Total persons	**620**	**100**	**160**	**26**	**100**	***74**	***12**	***100**	**143**	**23**	**100**
Population Density of Residence											
Urban.	441	71	115	26	72	*55	*12	*74	101	23	71
Rural	180	29	*45	*25	*28	...	...	...	*41	*23	*29
Population Size of Residence											
Metropolitan statistical areas											
(MSA).	534	86	152	28	95	*68	*13	*92	137	26	96
1,000,000 or more	144	23	...	...	...	...	...	...	...	...	...
250,000 to 999,999.	165	27	*67	*41	*42	...	...	...	*63	*38	*44
Less than 250,000.	224	36	*74	*33	*46	*41	*18	*56	*68	*30	*47
Outside MSA	87	14	...	...	...	...	...	...	...	...	...
Sex											
Male	309	50	*85	*27	*53	*35	*11	*48	*83	*27	*58
Female.	311	50	*75	*24	*47	*38	*12	*52	*60	*19	*42
Age											
6 to 8 years.	187	30	*60	*32	*37	...	...	...	*56	*30	*39
9 to 11 years.	231	37	*50	*22	*31	*35	*15	*47	*39	*17	*27
12 to 15 years.	202	33	*50	*25	*31	...	...	...	*48	*24	*34
Ethnicity											
Hispanic	...	...	...	...	...	...	...	...	...	...	...
Non-Hispanic	616	99	158	26	99	*74	*12	*100	141	23	99
Race											
White.	361	58	101	28	63	*66	*18	*90	88	24	61
Black.	240	39	*51	*21	*32	...	...	...	...	...	...
All others	...	...	...	...	...	...	...	...	...	...	...
Annual Household Income											
Less than $10,000.	*56	*9	...	...	...	...	...	...	...	...	...
$10,000 to $19,999.	...	...	...	...	...	...	...	...	...	...	...
$20,000 to $29,999.	95	15	...	...	...	...	...	...	...	...	...
$30,000 to $39,999.	86	14	...	...	...	...	...	...	...	...	...
$40,000 to $49,999.	*34	*6	...	...	...	...	...	...	...	...	...
$50,000 to $74,999.	137	22	*44	*32	*28	...	...	...	*44	*32	*31
$75,000 or more	109	18	*41	*38	*26	*34	*31	*46	*35	*33	*25
Not reported	69	11	...	...	...	...	...	...	...	...	...

* Estimate based on a sample size of 10–29.   ... Sample size too small to report data reliably.

Note: Percent who participated shows the percent of each row's population who participated in the activity named by the column (the percent of those living in urban areas who wildlife watched, etc.). Remaining percent columns show the percent of each column's participants who are described by the row heading (the percent of wildlife watchers who lived in urban areas, etc.). Data reported on this table are from screening interviews in which one adult household member responded for household members 6 to 15 years old. The screening interview required the respondent to recall 12 months' worth of activity. Includes state residents who wildlife watched only in other countries.

Appendix C

Appendix C.
Significant Methodological Changes From Previous Surveys and Regional Trends

This appendix provides a description of data collection changes and national and regional trend information based on the 1991, 1996, 2001, and 2006 Surveys. Since these four surveys used similar methodologies, their published information is directly comparable.

Significant Methodological Differences

The most significant design differences in the four surveys are as follows:

1. The 1991 Survey data were collected by interviewers filling out paper questionnaires. The data entries were keyed in a separate operation after the interview. The 1996, 2001, and 2006 Survey data were collected by the use of computer-assisted interviews. The questionnaires were programmed into computers, and the interviewer keyed in the responses at the time of the interview.

2. The 1991 Survey screening phase was conducted in January and February 1991, when the sample households were contacted and a household respondent was interviewed on behalf of the entire household. The screening interviews for the 1996, 2001, and 2006 Surveys were conducted April through June of their survey years in conjunction with the first wave of the detailed interviews. The screening interviews for all four surveys consisted primarily of demographic questions and wildlife-related recreation questions concerning activity in the previous year (1990, 1995, etc.) and intentions for recreating in the survey year.

In the 1991 Survey, an attempt was made to contact every sample person in all three detailed interview waves. In 1996, 2001, and 2006, respondents who were interviewed in the first detailed interview wave were not contacted again until the third wave. Also, all interviews in the second wave were conducted by telephone. In-person interviews were only conducted in the first and third waves.

Section I. Important Instrument Changes in the 1996 Survey

1. The 1991 Survey collected information on all wildlife-related recreation purchases made by participants without reference to where the purchase was made. The 1996 Survey asked in which state the purchase was made.

2. In 1991, respondents were asked what kind of fishing they did, i.e., Great Lakes, other freshwater, or saltwater, and then were asked in what states they fished. In 1996, respondents were asked in which states they fished and then were asked what kind of fishing they did. This method had the advantage of not asking about, for example, saltwater fishing when they only fished in a noncoastal state.

3. In 1991, respondents were asked how many days they "actually" hunted or fished for a particular type of game or fish and then how many days they "chiefly" hunted or fished for the same type of game or fish rather than another type of game or fish. To get total days of hunting or fishing for a particular type of game or fish, the "actually" day response was used, while to get the sum of all days of hunting or fishing, the "chiefly" days were summed. In 1996, respondents were asked their total days of hunting or fishing in the country and each state, then how many days

they hunted or fished for a particular type of game or fish.

4. Trip-related and equipment expenditure categories were not the same for all Surveys. "Guide fee" and "Pack trip or package fee" were two separate trip-related expenditure items in 1991, while they were combined into one category in the 1996 Survey. "Boating costs" was added to the 1996 hunting and wildlife-watching trip-related expenditure sections. "Heating and cooking fuel" was added to all of the trip-related expenditure sections. "Spearfishing equipment" was moved from a separate category to the "other" list. "Rods" and "Reels" were two separate categories in 1991 but were combined in 1996. "Lines, hooks, sinkers, etc." was one category in 1991 but split into "Lines" and "Hooks, sinkers, etc." in 1996. "Food used to feed other wildlife" was added to the wildlife-watching equipment section; "Boats" and "Cabins" were added to the wildlife-watching special equipment section; and "Land leasing and ownership" was added to the wildlife-watching expenditures section.

5. Questions asking sportspersons if they participated as much as they wanted were added in 1996. If the sportspersons said no, they were asked why not.

6. The 1991 Survey included questions about participation in organized fishing competitions; anglers using bows and arrows, nets or seines, or spearfishing; hunters using pistols or handguns and target shooting in preparation for hunting. These questions were not asked in 1996.

7. The 1996 Survey included questions about catch and release fishing and persons with disabilities participating in wildlife-related recreation. These questions were not part of the 1991 Survey.

8. The 1991 Survey included questions about average distance traveled to recreation sites. These questions were not included in the 1996 Survey.

9. The 1996 Survey included questions about the last trip the respondent took. Included were questions about the type of trip, where the activity took place, and the distance and direction to the site visited. These questions were not asked in 1991.

10. The 1991 Survey collected data on hunting, fishing, and wildlife watching by U.S. residents in Canada. The 1996 Survey collected data on fishing and wildlife watching by U.S. residents in Canada.

Section II. Important Instrument Changes in the 2001 Survey

1. The 1991 and 1996 single-race category "Asian or Pacific Islander" was changed to two categories— "Asian" and "Native Hawaiian or Other Pacific Islander." In 1991 and 1996, the respondent was required to pick only one category, while in 2001 the respondent could pick any combination of categories. The next question stipulated that the respondent could only be identified with one category and then asked what that category was.

2. The 1991 and 1996 land leasing and ownership sections asked the respondent to combine the two types of land use into one and give total acreage and expenditures. In 2001, the two types of land use were explored separately.

3. The 1991 and 1996 wildlife-watching sections included questions on birdwatching for residential users only. The 2001 Survey added a question on birdwatching for nonresidential users. Also, questions on the use of birding life lists

and how many species the respondent can identify were added.

4. "Recreational vehicles" was added to the sportspersons and wildlife-watchers special equipment section. "House trailer" was added to the sportspersons special equipment section.

5. Total personal income was asked in the detailed phase of the 1996 Survey. This was changed to total household income in the 2001 Survey.

6. A question was added to the trip-related expenditures section to ascertain how much of the total was spent in the respondent's state of residence when the respondent participated in hunting, fishing, or wildlife watching out of state.

7. Boating questions were added to the fishing section. The respondent was asked about the extent of boat usage for the three types of fishing.

8. The 1996 Survey included questions about the months residential wildlife watchers fed birds. These questions were not repeated in the 2001 Survey.

9. The contingent valuation sections of the three types of wildlife-related recreation were altered, using an open-ended question format instead of the dichotomous choice format used in 1996.

Section III. Important Instrument Changes in the 2006 Survey

1. A series of boating questions was added. The new questions dealt with anglers using motorboats and/or non-motorboats, length of boat used most often, distance to boat launch used most often, needed improvements to facilities at the launch, whether or not the respondent completed a boating safety course, who the boater fished with most often, and the source and type of information the boater used for his or her fishing.

2. Questions regarding catch and release fishing were added. Whether or not the respondent

caught and released fish and, if so, the percent of fish released.

3. The proportion of hunting done with a rifle or shotgun, as contrasted with muzzleloader or archery equipment, was asked.

4. In the contingent valuation section, where the value of wildlife-related recreation was determined, two quality-variable questions were added: the average length of certain fish caught and whether a deer, elk, or moose was killed. Plus, the economic evaluation bid questions were rephrased, from "What is the most your [species] hunting in [State name] could have cost you per trip last year before you would NOT have gone [species] hunting at all in 2001, not even one trip, because it would have been too expensive?," for the hunters, for example, to "What is the cost that would have prevented you from taking even one such trip in 2006? In other words, if the trip cost was below this amount, you would have gone [species] hunting in [State name], but if the trip cost was above this amount, you would not have gone."

5. Questions concerning hunting, fishing, or wildlife watching in other countries were taken out of the Survey.

6. Questions about the reasons for not going hunting or fishing, or not going as much as expected, were deleted.

7. Disability of participants questions were taken out.

8. Determination of the types of sites for wildlife watching was discontinued.

9. The birding questions regarding the use of birding life lists and the ability to identify birds based on their sight or sounds were deleted.

10. Public transportation costs were divided into two sections, "public transportation by airplane" and "other public transportation, including trains, buses, and car rentals, etc."

National and Regional Trends

Fishing and Hunting

Comparing national hunting and fishing estimates for 1991 to 2006 finds participation declining over the entire time period. In 1991 and 1996, the number of people who hunted and fished remained essentially unchanged. In 2001, the number of sportspersons fell compared to the two previous survey estimates. In 2006, the number of anglers continued to decline and the number of hunters was stable.

The amount of time people spent fishing and hunting fluctuated between 1991 and 2006. The number of days spent fishing rose 22 percent between 1991 and 1996, fell 11 percent between 1996 and 2001, and fell 7 percent further between 2001 and 2006. Days of hunting followed a similar pattern. Between 1991 and 1996, hunting days increased 9 percent (although this increase was not statistically significant) but then fell 11 percent between 1996 and 2001 and a further 4 percent (this was not statistically significant either) between 2001 and 2006.

The amount of money spent for fishing and hunting trips and equipment rose from 1991 to 1996, fell from 1996 to 2001, and stayed level from 2001 to 2006. The comparisons are in constant dollars.

Wildlife Watching

There were differing trend lines from 1991 to 2006 for the two major types of wildlife watching. The number of overall wildlife watchers decreased 17 percent from 1991 to 1996, increased 5 percent from 1996 to 2001, and increased 8 percent from 2001 to 2006. Around-the-home wildlife watching, the most popular type of wildlife watching, led this trend with an 18 percent drop from 1991 to 1996, a 4 percent increase from 1996 to 2001, and an 8 percent increase from 2001 to 2006. Away-from-home wildlife watching, on the other hand, dropped from 1991 to 2001 (21 percent from 1991 to 1996 and 8 percent from 1996 to 2001) and stayed level with a statistically insignificant 5 percent increase from 2001 to 2006. Days afield by away-from-home wildlife watchers were significantly up from 1996 to 2001 and statistically stable the other time periods. Overall expenditures for wildlife watching increased 21 percent from 1991 to 1996 and 16 percent from 1996 to 2001 and decreased a statistically insignificant 7 percent from 2001 to 2006.

Table C-1a. Comparison of Wildlife-Related Recreation in the United States: 1991–1996

(U.S. population 16 years old and older. Numbers in thousands. All expenditures in 2006 dollars. 1996 expenditure categories made comparable to 1991)

Participants, days, and expenditures	1991 (Number)	1996 (Number)	1991–1996 percent change
Hunting			
Hunters, total	14,063	13,975	−1*
Hunting days, total..	235,806	256,676	9*
Hunting expenditures, total	$18,282,597	$26,224,069	43
Fishing			
Anglers, total	35,578	35,246	−1*
Fishing days, total	511,329	625,893	22
Fishing expenditures, total.......................................	$35,553,365	$48,598,400	37
Wildlife Watching			
Wildlife watchers, total	76,111	62,868	−17
Around the home..	73,904	60,751	−18
Away from home...	29,999	23,652	−21
Wildlife-watching days, away from home	342,406	313,790	−8*
Wildlife-watching expenditures, total	$27,402,180	$33,093,660	21

* Not different from zero at the 5 percent level of significance.

Table C-1b. Comparison of Wildlife-Related Recreation in the United States: 1996–2001

(U.S. population 16 years old and older. Numbers in thousands. All expenditures in 2006 dollars. 1996 and 2001 expenditure categories made comparable to 1991)

Participants, days, and expenditures	1996 (Number)	2001 (Number)	1996–2001 percent change
Hunting			
Hunters, total	13,975	13,034	−7
Hunting days, total..	256,676	228,368	−11
Hunting expenditures, total	$26,224,069	$23,296,904	−11*
Fishing			
Anglers, total	35,246	34,071	−3
Fishing days, total	625,893	557,394	−11
Fishing expenditures, total.......................................	$48,598,400	$40,399,711	−17
Wildlife Watching			
Wildlife watchers, total	62,868	66,105	5
Around the home..	60,751	62,928	4
Away from home...	23,652	21,823	−8
Wildlife-watching days, away from home	313,790	372,006	19
Wildlife-watching expenditures, total	$33,093,660	$38,453,190	16

* Not different from zero at the 5 percent level of significance.

Table C-1c. Comparison of Wildlife-Related Recreation in the United States: 2001–2006

(U.S. population 16 years old and older. Numbers in thousands. All expenditures in 2006 dollars. 2001 and 2006 expenditure categories made comparable to 1991)

Participants, days, and expenditures	2001 (Number)	2006 (Number)	2001–2006 percent change
Hunting			
Hunters, total	13,034	12,510	−4*
Hunting days, total.	228,368	219,925	−4*
Hunting expenditures, total	$23,296,904	$22,644,048	−3*
Fishing			
Anglers, total	34,071	29,952	−12
Fishing days, total	557,394	516,781	−7
Fishing expenditures, total.	$40,399,711	$42,042,188	4*
Wildlife Watching			
Wildlife watchers, total	66,105	71,132	8
Around the home.	62,928	67,756	8
Away from home	21,823	22,977	5*
Wildlife-watching days, away from home	372,006	352,070	−5*
Wildlife-watching expenditures, total	$38,453,190	$35,870,403	−7*

* Not different from zero at the 5 percent level of significance.

Table C-1d. Comparison of Wildlife-Related Recreation in the United States: 1991–2006

(U.S. population 16 years old and older. Numbers in thousands. All expenditures in 2006 dollars. 2006 expenditure categories made comparable to 1991)

Participants, days, and expenditures	1991 (Number)	2006 (Number)	1991–2006 percent change
Hunting			
Hunters, total	14,063	12,510	−11
Hunting days, total.	235,806	219,925	−7*
Hunting expenditures, total	$18,282,597	$22,644,048	24
Fishing			
Anglers, total	35,578	29,952	−16
Fishing days, total	511,329	516,781	1*
Fishing expenditures, total.	$35,553,365	$42,042,188	18
Wildlife Watching			
Wildlife watchers, total	76,111	71,132	−7
Around the home.	73,904	67,756	−8
Away from home	29,999	22,977	−23
Wildlife-watching days, away from home	342,406	352,070	3*
Wildlife-watching expenditures, total	$27,402,180	$35,870,403	31

* Not different from zero at the 5 percent level of significance.

Table C-2. Anglers and Hunters by Census Division: 1991, 1996, 2001, and 2006

(U.S. population 16 years old and older. Numbers in thousands)

Area and sportsperson	1991 Number	1991 Percent	1996 Number	1996 Percent	2001 Number	2001 Percent	2006 Number	2006 Percent
UNITED STATES								
Total population	189,964	100	201,472	100	212,298	100	229,245	100
Sportspersons	39,979	21	39,694	20	37,805	18	33,916	15
Anglers	35,578	19	35,246	17	34,067	16	29,952	13
Hunters	14,063	7	13,975	7	13,034	6	12,510	5
New England								
Total population	10,180	100	10,306	100	10,575	100	11,233	100
Sportspersons	1,658	16	1,673	16	1,504	14	1,353	12
Anglers	1,545	15	1,520	15	1,402	13	1,246	11
Hunters	444	4	465	5	386	4	374	3
Middle Atlantic								
Total population	29,216	100	29,371	100	29,806	100	31,518	100
Sportspersons	4,508	15	4,192	14	3,810	13	3,214	10
Anglers	3,871	13	3,627	12	3,250	11	2,550	8
Hunters	1,746	6	1,453	5	1,633	5	1,520	5
East North Central								
Total population	32,188	100	33,121	100	34,082	100	35,609	100
Sportspersons	7,202	22	6,912	21	6,400	19	5,975	17
Anglers	6,264	19	6,006	18	5,655	17	5,190	15
Hunters	2,789	9	2,712	8	2,421	7	2,376	7
West North Central								
Total population	13,504	100	13,875	100	14,430	100	15,458	100
Sportspersons	4,143	31	3,977	29	4,239	29	3,836	25
Anglers	3,647	27	3,416	25	3,836	27	3,284	21
Hunters	1,709	13	1,917	14	1,710	12	1,779	12
South Atlantic								
Total population	33,682	100	36,776	100	39,286	100	43,965	100
Sportspersons	6,996	21	7,282	20	6,957	18	6,633	15
Anglers	6,441	19	6,636	18	6,451	16	6,116	14
Hunters	2,083	6	2,050	6	1,875	5	1,884	4
East South Central								
Total population	11,667	100	12,459	100	12,976	100	13,722	100
Sportspersons	2,984	26	2,907	23	2,865	22	2,689	20
Anglers	2,635	23	2,514	20	2,543	20	2,436	18
Hunters	1,279	11	1,301	10	1,164	9	1,101	8
West South Central								
Total population	19,926	100	21,811	100	23,337	100	25,407	100
Sportspersons	5,125	26	5,093	23	4,924	21	4,499	18
Anglers	4,592	23	4,616	21	4,375	19	3,952	16
Hunters	1,843	9	1,812	8	1,988	9	1,810	7
Mountain								·
Total population	10,092	100	11,966	100	13,308	100	15,651	100
Sportspersons	2,488	25	2,761	23	2,757	21	2,372	15
Anglers	2,079	21	2,411	20	2,443	18	2,084	13
Hunters	1,069	11	1,061	9	1,020	8	868	6
Pacific								
Total population	29,508	100	31,787	100	34,498	100	36,681	100
Sportspersons	4,875	17	4,897	15	4,349	13	3,345	9
Anglers	4,505	15	4,501	14	4,111	12	3,094	8
Hunters	1,101	4	1,203	4	837	2	798	2

Table C-3. Wildlife-Watching Participants by Census Division: 1991, 1996, 2001, and 2006

(Numbers in thousands. Population 16 years old and older)

Area and wildlife watcher	1991 Number	1991 Percent	1996 Number	1996 Percent	2001 Number	2001 Percent	2006 Number	2006 Percent
UNITED STATES								
Total population	189,964	100	201,472	100	212,298	100	229,245	100
Total wildlife watchers	76,111	40	62,868	31	66,105	31	71,132	31
Away from home	29,999	16	23,652	12	21,823	10	22,977	10
Around the home	73,904	39	60,751	30	62,928	30	67,756	30
New England								
Total population	10,180	100	10,306	100	10,575	100	11,233	100
Total wildlife watchers	4,598	45	3,710	36	3,875	37	4,489	40
Away from home	1,856	18	1,443	14	1,155	11	1,340	12
Around the home	4,544	45	3,586	35	3,765	36	4,310	38
Middle Atlantic								
Total population	29,216	100	29,371	100	29,806	100	31,518	100
Total wildlife watchers	10,556	36	8,185	28	8,740	29	8,723	28
Away from home	4,166	14	2,960	10	2,849	10	2,729	9
Around the home	10,282	35	8,023	27	8,452	28	8,451	27
East North Central								
Total population	32,188	100	33,121	100	34,082	100	35,609	100
Total wildlife watchers	14,511	45	11,731	35	11,631	34	12,215	34
Away from home	5,572	17	4,501	14	3,571	10	3,792	11
Around the home	14,175	44	11,297	34	11,196	33	11,845	33
West North Central								
Total population	13,504	100	13,875	100	14,430	100	15,458	100
Total wildlife watchers	6,924	51	5,089	37	6,206	43	6,741	44
Away from home	2,654	20	1,927	14	2,059	14	2,163	14
Around the home	6,722	50	4,900	35	5,938	41	6,447	42
South Atlantic								
Total population	33,682	100	36,776	100	39,286	100	43,965	100
Total wildlife watchers	13,047	39	11,252	31	11,395	29	12,862	29
Away from home	4,450	13	3,992	11	3,469	9	3,208	7
Around the home	12,813	38	10,964	30	10,911	28	12,432	28
East South Central								
Total population	11,667	100	12,459	100	12,976	100	13,722	100
Total wildlife watchers	4,864	42	3,904	31	4,514	35	4,931	36
Away from home	1,592	14	1,118	9	1,086	8	1,758	13
Around the home	4,765	41	3,795	30	4,390	34	4,683	34
West South Central								
Total population	19,926	100	21,811	100	23,337	100	25,407	100
Total wildlife watchers	7,035	35	5,933	27	5,747	25	6,764	27
Away from home	2,459	12	2,096	10	1,822	8	2,127	8
Around the home	6,817	34	5,773	26	5,490	24	6,319	25
Mountain								
Total population	10,092	100	11,966	100	13,308	100	15,651	100
Total wildlife watchers	4,437	44	4,099	34	4,619	35	4,968	32
Away from home	2,215	22	1,967	16	2,019	15	2,004	13
Around the home	4,145	41	3,855	32	4,282	32	4,605	29
Pacific								
Total population	29,508	100	31,787	100	34,498	100	36,681	100
Total wildlife watchers	10,139	34	8,966	28	9,377	27	9,439	26
Away from home	5,035	17	3,648	11	3,793	11	3,856	11
Around the home	9,641	33	8,558	27	8,504	25	8,664	24

Appendix D

Appendix D.
Sample Design and Statistical Accuracy

This appendix is presented in two parts. The first part is the U.S. Census Bureau Source and Accuracy Statement. This statement describes the sampling design for the 2006 Survey and highlights the steps taken to produce estimates from the completed questionnaires. The statement explains the use of standard errors and confidence intervals. It also provides comprehensive information about errors characteristic of surveys and formulas and parameters to calculate an approximate standard error or confidence interval for each number published in this report. The second part reports approximate standard errors for selected measures of participation and expenditures for wildlife-related recreation. Tables D-1 to D-3 show common estimates by state with their estimated standard errors. Tables D-4 to D-9 provide parameters for computing standard errors.

Source and Accuracy Statement for the Louisiana State Report of the *2006 National Survey of Fishing, Hunting, and Wildlife-Associated Recreation*

SOURCE OF DATA

The estimates in this report are based on data collected in the *2006 National Survey of Fishing, Hunting, and Wildlife-Associated Recreation* (FHWAR) conducted by the Census Bureau and sponsored by the U.S. Fish and Wildlife Service.

The eligible universe for the FHWAR is the civilian noninstitutionalized and nonbarrack military population living in the United States. The institutionalized population, which is excluded from the population universe, is composed primarily of the population in correctional institutions and nursing homes (91 percent of the 4.1 million institutionalized people in Census 2000).

The 2006 Survey was designed to provide state-level estimates of the number of participants in recreational hunting and fishing and in wildlife-watching activities (e.g., wildlife observation). Information was collected on the number of participants, where and how often they participated, the type of wildlife encountered, and the amounts of money spent on wildlife-related recreation.

The Survey was conducted in two stages: an initial screening of households to identify likely sportspersons and wildlife-watching participants and a series of follow-up interviews of selected persons to collect detailed data about their wildlife-related recreation during 2006.

SAMPLE DESIGN

The 2006 FHWAR sample was selected from the Census Bureau's master address file (MAF) and unused sample of the Current Population Survey (CPS). The CPS sample was used to improve coverage in rural areas of some states.

The FHWAR is a multistage probability sample, with coverage in all 50 states and the District of Columbia. In the first stage of the sampling process, primary sampling units (PSUs) are selected for sample. The PSUs are defined to correspond to the Office of Management and Budget definitions of Core Based Statistical Area definitions and to improve efficiency in field operations. The United States is divided into 2,025 PSUs. These PSUs are grouped into 824 strata. Within each stratum, a single PSU is chosen for the sample, with its probability of selection proportional to its population as of the most recent decennial census. This PSU represents the entire stratum from which it was selected. In the case of strata consisting of only one PSU, the PSU is chosen with certainty.

Within the selected PSUs, the FHWAR sample was selected from the MAF where sufficient coverage of addresses existed. In some rural areas, the sample was selected from unused cases from the CPS to improve coverage.

FHWAR Screening Sample

The total screening sample in Louisiana consisted of **1,225** households. Interviewing for the screen was conducted during April, May, and June 2006. Of all housing units in sample, about **970** were determined to be eligible for interview. Interviewers obtained interviews at **902** of these units for a state response rate of **93** percent. Local field representatives conducted interviews by telephone when possible, otherwise through a personal visit. The field representatives asked screening questions for all household members 6 years old and older. Noninterviews occur when the occupants are not found at home after repeated calls or are unavailable for some other reason.

Data for the FHWAR sportspersons sample and wildlife-watchers sample were collected in three waves. The first wave started in April 2006, the second in September 2006, and the third in January 2007. In the sportspersons sample, all persons who hunted or fished in 2006 by the time of the screening interview were interviewed in the first wave. The remaining sportspersons in sample were interviewed in the second wave. A subsampling operation was conducted before the third wave of sampling to reduce cost of the Survey, and everyone remaining in sample was interviewed in the third wave.

The reference period was the preceding 4 months for waves 1 and 2. In wave 3, the reference period was either 4, 8, or 12 months depending on when the sample person was first interviewed.

Detailed Samples

Two independent detailed samples were chosen from the FHWAR screening sample. One consisted of sportspersons (people who hunt or fish) and the other of wildlife watchers (people who observe, photograph, or feed wildlife).

A. Sportspersons

The Census Bureau selected the detailed samples based on information reported during the screening phase. Based on information collected from the household respondent, every person 16 years old and older in the FHWAR screening sample was assigned to a sportspersons stratum. The criteria for the strata included time devoted to hunting or fishing in previous years, participation in hunting or fishing in 2006 by the time of the screening interview, and intentions to participate in hunting and fishing activities during the remainder of 2006. The four sportspersons categories were:

1. *Active*—a person who had already participated in hunting or fishing in 2006 at the time of the screener interview.

2. *Likely*—a person who had not participated in 2006 at the time of the screener, but had participated in 2005 OR was likely to participate in 2006.

3. *Inactive*—a person who had not participated in 2005 or 2006 AND was somewhat unlikely to participate in 2006.

4. *Nonparticipant*—a person who had not participated in 2005 or 2006 AND was very unlikely to participate in 2006.

Persons were selected for the detailed phase based on these groupings.

Active sportspersons were given the detailed interview twice—at the time of the screening interview (in April, May, or June 2006) and again in January or February 2007. Likely sportspersons and a subsample of the inactive sportspersons were also interviewed twice—first in September or October 2006,

then in January or February 2007. If Census Bureau field representatives were not able to obtain the first interview, they attempted to interview the person in the final interviewing period with the reference period being the entire year. Persons in the nonparticipant group were not eligible for a detailed interview.

About **440** persons were designated for interviews in Louisiana. The detailed sportspersons sample sizes varied by state to get reliable state-level estimates. During each interview period, about **22** percent of the designated persons were not found at home or were unavailable for some other reason. Overall, about **343** detailed sportspersons interviews were completed at a response rate of **78** percent.

B. Wildlife Watchers

The wildlife-watching detailed sample was also selected based on information reported during the screening phase. Based on information collected from the household respondent, every person 16 years old and older was assigned to a stratum. The criteria for the strata included time devoted to wildlife-watching activities in previous years, participation in wildlife-watching activities in 2006 by the time of the screening interview, and intentions to participate in wildlife-watching activities during the remainder of 2006. The five wildlife-watching categories were:

1. *Active*—a person who had already participated in 2006 at the time of the screening interview.

2. *Avid*—a person who had not yet participated in 2006, but in 2005 had taken trips to participate in wildlife-watching activities for 21 or more days or had spent $300 or more.

3. *Average*—a person who had not yet participated in 2006, but in 2005 had taken trips to wildlife watch for less than 21 days and had spent less than $300 OR had not participated in wildlife-watching activities but was very

likely to in the remainder of 2006.

4. *Infrequent*—a person who had not participated in 2005 or 2006, but was somewhat likely or somewhat unlikely to participate in the remainder of 2006.

5. *Nonparticipant*—a person who had not participated in 2005 or 2006 AND was very unlikely to participate during the remainder of 2006.

Persons were selected for the detailed sample based on these groupings, but persons in the nonparticipant group were not eligible for a detailed interview. A subsample of each of the other groups was selected to receive a detailed interview with the chance of selection diminishing as the likelihood of participation diminished.

Wildlife-watching participants were given the detailed interview twice. Some received their first detailed interview at the same time as the screening interview (in April, May, or June 2006). The rest received their first detailed interview in September or October 2006. All wildlife-watching participants received their second interview in January or February 2007. If Census Bureau field representatives were not able to obtain the first interview, they attempted to interview the person in the final interviewing period with the reference period being the entire year.

About **150** persons were designated for interviews in Louisiana. The detailed wildlife-watching sample sizes varied by state to get reliable state-level estimates. During each interview period, about **17** percent of the designated persons were not found at home or were unavailable for some other reason. Overall, about **124** detailed wildlife-watcher interviews were completed at a response rate of **83** percent.

ESTIMATION PROCEDURE

Several stages of adjustments were used to derive the final 2006 FHWAR person weights. A brief description of the major components of the weights is given next.

All statistics for the population 6 to 15 years of age were derived from the screening interview. Statistics for the population 16 years old and older come from both the screening and detailed interviews. Estimates that come from the screening sample are presented in Appendix B.

A. Screening Sample

Every interviewed person in the screening sample received a screening weight that was the product of the following factors:

1. *Base Weight.* The base weight is the inverse of the household's probability of selection.

2. *Household Noninterview Adjustment.* The noninterview adjustment inflates the weight assigned to interviewed households to account for households eligible for interview but for which no interview was obtained.

3. *First-Stage Adjustment.* The 824 areas designated for our samples were selected from 2,025 such areas of the United States. Some sample areas represent only themselves and are referred to as self-representing. The remaining areas represent other areas similar in selected characteristics and are thus designated non-self-representing. The first-stage factor reduces the component of variation arising from sampling the non-self-representing areas.

4. *Second-Stage Adjustment.* This adjustment brings the estimates of the total population into agreement with census-based estimates of the civilian noninstitutionalized and nonbarrack military populations for each state.

B. Sportspersons Sample

Every interviewed person in the sportspersons detailed sample received a weight that was the product of the following factors:

1. *Screening Weight.* This is the person's final weight from the screening sample.

2. *Sportspersons Stratum Adjustment.* This factor inflates the weights of persons selected for the detailed sample to account for the subsampling done within each sportsperson stratum.

3. *Sportspersons Noninterview Adjustment.* This factor adjusts the weights of the interviewed sportspersons to account for sportspersons selected for the detailed sample for whom no interview was obtained. A person was considered a noninterview if he or she was not interviewed in the third wave of interviewing.

4. *Sportspersons Ratio Adjustment Factor.* This is a ratio adjustment of the detailed sample to the screening sample within the sportspersons sampling stratum. This adjustment brings the population estimates of persons aged 16 years old and older from the detailed sample into agreement with the same estimates from the screening sample, which was a much larger sample.

C. Wildlife-Watchers Sample

Every interviewed person in the wildlife-watchers detailed sample received a weight that was the product of the following factors:

1. *Screening Weight.* This is the person's final weight from the screening sample.

2. *Wildlife-Watchers Stratum Adjustment.* This factor inflates the weights of persons selected for the detailed sample to account for the subsampling done within each wildlife-watcher stratum.

3. *Wildlife-Watchers Noninterview Adjustment.* This factor adjusts the weights of the interviewed wildlife-watching participants to account for wildlife watchers selected for the detailed sample for which no interview was obtained. A person was considered a noninterview if he or she was not interviewed in the third wave of interviewing.

4. *Wildlife-Watchers Ratio Adjustment Factor.* This is a ratio adjustment of the detailed sample to the screening sample within wildlife-watchers sampling strata. This adjustment brings the population estimates of persons aged 16 years old and older from the detailed sample into agreement with the same estimates from the screening sample, which was a much larger sample.

ACCURACY OF THE ESTIMATES

A sample survey estimate has two types of error: sampling and nonsampling. The accuracy of an estimate depends on both types of error. The nature of the sampling error is known given the survey design; the full extent of the nonsampling error is unknown.

NONSAMPLING ERROR

For a given estimator, the difference between the estimate that would result if the sample were to include the entire population and the true population value being estimated is known as nonsampling error. There are several sources of nonsampling error that may occur during the development or execution of the survey. It can occur because of circumstances created by the interviewer, the respondent, the survey instrument, or the way the data are collected and processed. For example, errors could occur because:

- The interviewer records the wrong answer, the respondent provides incorrect information, the respondent estimates the requested information, or an unclear survey question is misunderstood by the respondent (measurement error).

- Some individuals who should have been included in the survey frame were missed (coverage error).

- Responses are not collected from all those in the sample or the respondent is unwilling to provide information (nonresponse error).

- Values are estimated imprecisely for missing data (imputation error).

- Forms may be lost, data may be incorrectly keyed, coded, or recoded, etc. (processing error).

The Census Bureau employs quality control procedures throughout the production process, including the overall design of surveys, the wording of questions, the review of the work of interviewers and coders, and the statistical review of reports to minimize these errors.

Two types of nonsampling error that can be examined to a limited extent are nonresponse and undercoverage.

Nonresponse. The effect of nonresponse cannot be measured directly, but one indication of its potential effect is the nonresponse rate. For the FHWAR screener interview in Louisiana, the household-level nonresponse rate was 7 percent. The person-level nonresponse rate for the detailed sportsperson interview in Louisiana was an additional 22 percent and for the wildlife watchers it was 17 percent. Since the screener nonresponse rate is a household-level rate and the detailed interview nonresponse rate is a person-level rate, we cannot combine these rates to derive an overall nonresponse rate. Since it is unlikely the nonresponding households to the FHWAR have the same number of persons as the households successfully interviewed, combining these rates would result in an overestimate of the "true" person-level overall nonresponse rate for the detailed interviews.

Coverage. Overall screener undercoverage is estimated to be about 13 percent. Ratio estimation to independent population controls, as described previously, partially corrects for the bias due to survey undercoverage. However, biases exist in the estimates to the extent that missed persons in missed households or missed persons in interviewed households have different characteristics from those of interviewed persons in the same age group.

Comparability of Data. Data obtained from the 2006 FHWAR and other sources are not entirely comparable. This results from differences in interviewer training and experience and in differing survey processes. This is an example of nonsampling variability not reflected in the standard errors. Therefore, caution should be used when comparing results from different sources. (See Appendix C.)

A Nonsampling Error Warning. Since the full extent of the nonsampling error is unknown, one should be particularly careful when interpreting results based on small differences between estimates. The Census Bureau recommends that data users incorporate information about nonsampling errors into their analyses, as nonsampling error could impact the conclusions drawn from the results. Caution should also be used when interpreting results based on a relatively small number of cases. Summary measures (such as medians and percentage distributions) probably do not reveal useful information when computed on a subpopulation smaller than 50,000 for screener data, 65,000 for the detailed sportsperson data, and 230,000 for the wildlife-watchers data.

SAMPLING ERROR

Since the FHWAR estimates come from a sample, they may differ from figures from an enumeration of the entire population using the same questionnaires, instructions, and enumerators. For a given estimator, the difference between an estimate based on a sample and the estimate that would result if the sample were to include the entire population is known as sampling error. Standard errors, as calculated by methods described in "Standard Errors and Their Use," are primarily measures of the magnitude of sampling error. However, they may include some nonsampling error.

Standard Errors and Their Use. The sample estimate and its standard error enable one to construct a confidence interval. A confidence interval is a range that has a known probability of including the average result of all possible samples. For example, if all possible samples were surveyed under essentially the same general conditions and using the same sample design, and if an estimate and its standard error were calculated from each sample, then approximately 90 percent of the intervals from 1.645 standard errors below the estimate to 1.645 standard errors above the estimate would include the average result of all possible samples.

A particular confidence interval may or may not contain the average estimate derived from all possible samples. However, one can say with specified confidence that the interval includes the average estimate calculated from all possible samples.

Standard errors may also be used to perform hypothesis testing, a procedure for distinguishing between population parameters using sample estimates. The most common type of hypothesis is that the population parameters are different. An example would be comparing the proportion of anglers to the proportion of hunters.

Tests may be performed at various levels of significance. A significance level is the probability of concluding that the characteristics are different when, in fact, they are the same. For example, to conclude that two characteristics are different at the 0.1 level of significance, the absolute value of the estimated difference between characteristics must be greater than or equal to 1.645 times the standard error of the difference.

This report uses 90-percent confidence intervals and 0.1 level of significance to determine statistical validity. Consult standard statistical textbooks for alternative criteria.

Estimating Standard Errors. The Census Bureau uses replication methods to estimate the standard errors of FHWAR estimates. These methods primarily measure the magnitude of sampling error. However, they do measure some effects of nonsampling error as well. They do not measure systematic biases in the data associated with nonsampling error. Bias is the average over all possible samples of the differences between the sample estimates and the true value.

Generalized Variance Parameters. While it is possible to compute and present an estimate of the standard error based on the survey data for each estimate in a report, there are a number of reasons why this is not done. A presentation of the individual standard errors would be of limited use, since one could not possibly predict all of the combinations of results that may be of interest to data users. Additionally, data users have access to FHWAR microdata files, and it is impossible to compute in advance the standard error for every estimate one might obtain from those data sets. Moreover, variance estimates are based on sample data and have variances of their own. Therefore, some methods of stabilizing these estimates of variance, for example, by generalizing or averaging over time, may be used to improve their reliability.

Experience has shown that certain groups of estimates have similar relationships between their variances and expected values. Modeling or generalizing may provide more stable variance estimates by taking advantage of these similarities. The generalized variance function is a simple model that expresses the variance as a function of the expected value of the survey estimate. The parameters of the generalized variance function are estimated using direct replicate variances. These generalized variance parameters provide a relatively easy method to obtain approximate standard errors for numerous characteristics. Tables D-4 to D-9 provide the generalized variance parameters for FHWAR data. Methods for using the parameters to calculate standard errors of various estimates are given in the next sections.

Standard Errors of Estimated Numbers. The approximate standard error, s_x, of an estimated number shown in this report can be obtained using the following formulas. Formula (1) is used to calculate the standard errors of levels of sportspersons, anglers, and wildlife watchers.

$$s_x = \sqrt{ax^2 + bx} \tag{1}$$

Here, x is the size of the estimate and a and b are the parameters in the tables associated with the particular characteristic.

Formula (2) is used for standard errors of aggregates, i.e., trips, days, and expenditures.

$$s_x = \sqrt{ax^2 + bx + \frac{cx^2}{y}} \tag{2}$$

Here, x is again the size of the estimate; y is the base of the estimate; and a, b, and c are the parameters in the tables associated with the particular characteristic.

Illustration of the Computation of the Standard Error of an Estimated Number

Suppose there were an estimated 33,916,000 persons age 16 years old and older who either fished or hunted in the United States in 2006. Using formula (1) with the parameters a = –0.000027 and b = 6,125 from table D-5, the approximate standard error of the estimated number of 33,916,000 sportspersons age 16 years old and older is

$$s_x = \sqrt{-0.000027 \times 33,916,000^2 + 6,125 \times 33,916,000} = 420,330$$

The 90-percent confidence interval for the estimated number of sportspersons 16 years old and older is from 33,225,000 to 34,607,000, i.e., 33,916,000 ± 1.645 x 420,330. Therefore, a conclusion that the average estimate derived from all possible samples lies within a range computed in this way would be correct for roughly 90 percent of all possible samples.

Suppose there were an estimated 12,510,000 hunters aged 16 years old and older who engaged in 219,925,000 days of participation in 2006. Using formula (2) with the parameters a = –0.000235, b = –85,241, and c = 22,698 from table D-7, the approximate standard error on 219,925,000 estimated days on an estimated base of 12,510,000 hunters is

$$s_x = \sqrt{-0.000235 \times 219,925,000^2 - 85,241 \times 219,925,000 + \frac{22,698 \times 219,925,000^2}{12,510,000}} = 7,592,000$$

The 90-percent confidence interval on the estimate of 219,925,000 days is from 207,436,000 to 232,414,000, i.e., 219,925,000 ± 1.645 x 7,592,000. Again, a conclusion that the average estimate derived from all possible samples lies within a range computed in this way would be correct for roughly 90 percent of all possible samples.

Standard Errors of Estimated Percentages. The reliability of an estimated percentage, computed using sample data for both numerator and denominator, depends on the size of the percentage and its base. Estimated percentages are relatively more reliable than the corresponding estimates of the numerators of the percentages, particularly if the percentages are 50 percent or more. When the numerator and the denominator of the percentage are in different categories, use the parameter in the tables indicated by the numerator.

The approximate standard error, $s_{x,p}$, can be obtained by use of the formula

$$s_{x,p} = \sqrt{\frac{bp(100 - p)}{x}} \tag{3}$$

Here, x is the total number of sportspersons, hunters, etc., which is the base of the percentage; p is the percentage $(0 \leq p \leq 100)$; and b is the parameter in the tables associated with the characteristic in the numerator of the percentage.

Illustration of the Computation of the Standard Error of an Estimated Percentage

Suppose there were an estimated 12,510,000 hunters aged 16 years old and older of whom 18.3 percent hunted migratory birds. From table D-5, the appropriate b parameter is 5,756. Using formula (3), the approximate standard error on the estimate of 18.3 percent is

$$S_{x,p} = \sqrt{\frac{5{,}756 \times 18.3 \times (100 - 18.3)}{12{,}510{,}000}} = 0.83$$

Consequently, the 90-percent confidence interval for the estimate percentage of migratory bird hunters 16 years old and older is from 16.9 percent to 19.7 percent, i.e., $18.3 \pm 1.645 \times 0.83$.

Standard Error of a Difference. The standard error of the difference between two sample estimates is approximately equal to

$$S_{x-y} = \sqrt{s_x^2 + s_y^2} \qquad (4)$$

where s_x and s_y are the standard errors of the estimates x and y. The estimates can be numbers, percentages, ratios, etc. This will represent the actual standard error quite accurately for the difference between estimates of the same characteristic in two different areas, or for the difference between separate and uncorrelated characteristics in the same area. However, if there is a high positive (negative) correlation between the two characteristics, the formula will overestimate (underestimate) the true standard error.

Illustration of the Computation of the Standard Error of a Difference

Suppose there were an estimated 11,655,000 females in the age range of 18 to 24 of whom 726,000 or 6.2 percent were sportspersons. Similarly, suppose there were an estimated 11,638,000 males in the same age range of whom 1,929,000 or 16.6 percent were sportspersons. The apparent difference between the percentage of female and male sportspersons is 10.4 percent. Using formula (3) and the appropriate b parameter from table D-5, the approximate standard errors of 6.2 percent and 16.6 percent are 0.55 and 0.85, respectively. Using formula (4), the approximate standard error of the estimated difference of 10.4 percent is

$$S_{x-y} = \sqrt{0.55^2 + 0.85^2} = 1.02$$

The 90-percent confidence interval on the difference between 18-to-24-year-old female and male sportspersons is from 8.7 to 12.1, i.e., $10.4 \pm 1.645 \times 1.02$. Since the interval does not contain zero, we can conclude with 90-percent confidence that the percentage of 18-to-24-year-old female sportspersons is less than the percentage of 18-to-24-year-old male sportspersons.

Standard Errors of Estimated Averages. Certain mean values for sportspersons, anglers, etc., shown in the report were calculated as the ratio of two numbers. For example, average days per angler is calculated as:

$$\frac{x}{y} = \frac{total\ days}{total\ anglers}$$

Standard errors for these averages may be approximated by the use of formula (5) below.

$$S_{x/y} = \frac{x}{y} \sqrt{\left[\frac{s_x}{x}\right]^2 + \left[\frac{s_y}{y}\right]^2 - 2r\frac{s_x s_y}{xy}} \qquad (5)$$

In formula (5), r represents the correlation coefficient between the numerator and the denominator of the estimate. In the above formula, use 0.7 as an estimate of r.

Illustration of the Computation of the Standard Error of an Estimated Average

Suppose that the estimated number of the average days per angler aged 16 years old and older for all fishing was 17.3 days. Using formulas (1) and (2) above, we compute the standard error on total days, 516,781,000, and total anglers, 29,952,000, to be 15,828,079 and 399,342, respectively. The approximate standard error on the estimated average of 17.3 days is

$$
s_{x/y} = \frac{516,781,000}{29,952,000} \sqrt{\left[\frac{158,280,079}{516,781,000}\right]^2 + \left[\frac{399,342}{29,952,000}\right]^2 - 2 \times 0.7 \frac{15,828,079 \times 399,342}{516,781,000 \times 29,952,000}} = 0.40
$$

Therefore, the 90-percent confidence interval on the estimated average of 17.3 days is from 16.6 to 18.0, i.e., 17.3 ± 1.645 x 0.40.

Table D-1. Approximate Standard Errors of Resident Anglers, Days of Fishing by State Residents, and Expenditures for Fishing by State Residents

(Numbers in thousands)

State	Participation		Days		Expenditures in dollars	
	Estimate	Standard error	Estimate	Standard error	Estimate	Standard error
Alabama	628	41	13,164	2,463	791,187	136,335
Alaska	138	10	1,965	329	221,328	43,350
Arizona	370	32	4,378	1,163	293,510	62,037
Arkansas	463	38	10,078	1,788	364,528	71,945
California	1,689	102	19,649	2,646	2,707,995	428,592
Colorado	554	40	6,737	1,081	1,093,571	147,080
Connecticut	291	20	6,239	1,239	442,724	95,897
Delaware	76	6	1,521	397	138,601	28,408
Florida	1,950	100	43,026	5,370	3,618,499	514,463
Georgia	1,060	77	18,449	3,935	1,050,608	183,960
Hawaii	94	8	1,345	300	82,728	22,551
Idaho	223	22	4,126	1,222	234,363	52,127
Illinois	1,034	62	21,351	2,579	1,315,192	197,171
Indiana	739	50	10,583	1,315	696,389	128,034
Iowa	449	34	7,017	1,319	398,654	78,100
Kansas	369	27	5,643	916	299,896	63,027
Kentucky	622	45	9,874	1,600	963,254	239,107
Louisiana	598	47	11,075	1,337	807,063	153,792
Maine	225	17	3,854	800	147,473	26,410
Maryland	475	32	6,571	1,028	661,078	99,475
Massachusetts	452	29	9,309	1,784	954,647	229,603
Michigan	1,098	89	23,239	4,004	1,662,875	364,329
Minnesota	1,143	75	23,025	4,850	2,467,491	483,774
Mississippi	479	34	7,515	1,198	280,529	55,307
Missouri	931	59	16,227	2,889	1,032,407	160,090
Montana	179	16	2,455	424	140,895	27,916
Nebraska	192	15	3,208	532	217,437	36,020
Nevada	156	16	1,958	447	304,133	73,096
New Hampshire	124	10	2,488	442	141,041	27,264
New Jersey	530	33	9,237	1,601	1,167,944	196,789
New Mexico	190	18	2,451	838	254,023	76,563
New York	1,029	81	16,157	3,315	844,153	194,665
North Carolina	964	63	16,106	2,626	1,039,286	198,626
North Dakota	106	8	1,150	205	96,908	19,580
Ohio	1,293	91	17,583	3,199	1,118,439	226,342
Oklahoma	547	39	10,363	1,487	486,013	88,047
Oregon	483	39	8,104	2,308	507,625	101,717
Pennsylvania	990	87	20,592	4,258	1,625,022	272,116
Rhode Island	83	6	1,480	207	125,121	25,668
South Carolina	548	39	11,174	1,814	1,101,128	340,271
South Dakota	95	9	1,456	254	137,159	28,262
Tennessee	708	54	13,966	2,025	576,667	110,670
Texas	2,344	172	40,101	5,924	3,883,589	796,872
Utah	313	26	3,841	851	408,986	84,433
Vermont	71	7	1,506	279	59,132	12,200
Virginia	731	58	9,932	1,331	669,565	140,722
Washington	690	43	9,111	1,394	967,520	180,668
West Virginia	306	25	6,967	1,000	335,880	104,458
Wisconsin	1,025	66	17,771	2,431	1,193,390	201,965
Wyoming	98	10	1,360	282	450,339	133,641

Table D-2. Approximate Standard Errors of Resident Hunters, Days of Hunting by State Residents, and Expenditures for Hunting by State Residents

(Numbers in thousands)

State	Participation		Days		Expenditures in dollars	
	Estimate	Standard error	Estimate	Standard error	Estimate	Standard error
Alabama	312	30	8,032	1,831	596,485	114,760
Alaska	55	7	859	205	111,535	25,306
Arizona	129	15	1,535	405	360,537	108,628
Arkansas	307	31	7,630	1,629	765,599	146,698
California	317	43	4,192	1,041	960,932	230,698
Colorado	132	18	1,421	303	219,545	57,088
Connecticut	40	7	693	181	96,638	38,704
Delaware	21	3	512	148	33,836	7,761
Florida	325	40	5,723	1,200	870,391	205,731
Georgia	356	42	7,180	1,643	502,017	135,282
Hawaii	19	4	421	214	24,992	9,869
Idaho	123	15	1,187	256	142,708	33,385
Illinois	272	32	4,609	938	416,950	80,383
Indiana	254	30	4,617	930	243,058	60,232
Iowa	210	26	3,734	869	260,147	60,083
Kansas	192	23	2,717	723	231,228	58,822
Kentucky	261	29	5,108	637	507,473	116,274
Louisiana	275	33	7,155	1,443	618,264	142,285
Maine	146	14	2,042	319	211,434	40,017
Maryland	151	17	2,213	399	230,214	44,830
Massachusetts	66	11	1,629	562	238,670	98,246
Michigan	721	79	11,756	2,256	846,455	202,158
Minnesota	536	53	6,947	1,571	752,098	171,270
Mississippi	244	24	6,227	820	446,639	89,602
Missouri	560	49	9,685	1,876	1,027,698	167,223
Montana	145	14	1,817	315	219,465	46,679
Nebraska	105	13	1,647	349	176,456	33,615
Nevada	60	10	687	249	149,750	51,854
New Hampshire	52	6	1,037	206	77,932	19,911
New Jersey	84	12	1,621	342	160,737	44,444
New Mexico	72	11	734	240	109,297	35,712
New York	502	52	9,734	1,927	835,147	258,055
North Carolina	304	34	5,428	1,059	688,691	160,961
North Dakota	86	8	1,125	207	92,576	18,993
Ohio	477	53	10,728	2,771	863,874	214,994
Oklahoma	232	28	5,556	1,209	463,726	95,364
Oregon	219	24	2,768	718	336,278	69,062
Pennsylvania	933	92	17,401	2,585	1,581,058	276,321
Rhode Island	13	2	184	45	13,766	4,278
South Carolina	166	23	4,025	1,294	253,796	115,579
South Dakota	90	8	1,208	233	87,120	15,955
Tennessee	284	34	6,318	1,224	481,767	114,181
Texas	996	108	13,896	1,937	2,048,671	462,353
Utah	154	18	1,884	530	332,629	76,446
Vermont	57	6	1,068	157	69,059	15,885
Virginia	360	47	6,649	1,156	493,125	110,305
Washington	187	25	2,385	563	389,792	117,244
West Virginia	200	21	3,602	578	325,688	116,172
Wisconsin	652	53	9,998	1,316	1,329,161	272,105
Wyoming	52	6	604	149	89,832	29,427

Table D-3. Approximate Standard Errors of Resident Away-From-Home Participants, Days of Away-From-Home Participants by State Residents, and Trip-Related Expenditures for Away-From-Home Activities by State Residents

(Numbers in thousands)

State	Participation		Days		Expenditures in dollars	
	Estimate	Standard error	Estimate	Standard error	Estimate	Standard error
Alabama	348	50	7,301	3,047	198,132	61,485
Alaska	68	13	1,492	520	65,576	27,602
Arizona	381	42	4,554	886	301,997	75,465
Arkansas	304	46	4,253	1,372	70,098	25,680
California	2,565	200	46,538	8,681	2,226,634	504,935
Colorado	531	67	7,548	1,984	303,943	83,737
Connecticut	290	33	4,987	1,043	240,708	61,745
Delaware	49	8	811	276	12,490	3,833
Florida	988	119	13,180	3,390	455,521	105,349
Georgia	371	71	4,934	1,761	289,920	122,816
Hawaii	55	10	485	124	30,005	10,851
Idaho	183	32	2,876	805	87,351	28,403
Illinois	756	92	7,366	1,477	431,477	115,300
Indiana	611	72	7,894	1,650	234,756	61,310
Iowa	344	51	4,233	867	104,542	33,072
Kansas	234	31	3,427	1,156	91,838	28,745
Kentucky	540	68	3,978	835	163,835	45,402
Louisiana	234	42	3,536	1,038	118,317	49,801
Maine	213	30	3,938	1,066	105,340	28,268
Maryland	305	43	4,841	1,310	103,265	25,729
Massachusetts	531	50	8,959	1,720	249,979	56,447
Michigan	827	127	10,455	3,288	522,877	153,343
Minnesota	579	92	9,010	2,413	458,934	162,740
Mississippi	145	35	1,391	421	77,767	27,913
Missouri	709	86	14,619	3,543	365,259	103,690
Montana	184	23	1,777	498	57,461	20,990
Nebraska	151	18	1,201	176	55,793	15,941
Nevada	168	26	1,912	479	108,053	42,601
New Hampshire	127	16	2,246	561	61,263	14,140
New Jersey	513	54	8,408	2,189	195,252	44,467
New Mexico	220	24	3,803	844	81,860	20,074
New York	1,178	147	13,927	2,835	887,039	240,941
North Carolina	402	59	3,544	1,035	324,968	105,504
North Dakota	30	8	278	120	8,290	3,921
Ohio	1,174	125	9,232	1,427	365,635	95,003
Oklahoma	414	60	7,930	3,634	291,664	81,739
Oregon	481	66	7,455	3,205	177,364	51,932
Pennsylvania	1,038	127	13,013	2,727	587,806	168,911
Rhode Island	96	10	1,207	293	44,400	11,412
South Carolina	332	46	2,222	471	167,464	44,431
South Dakota	116	17	709	143	46,769	14,583
Tennessee	725	82	14,819	4,776	242,507	73,041
Texas	1,176	206	31,689	12,769	922,669	360,407
Utah	255	36	3,063	817	116,401	32,391
Vermont	82	11	1,803	504	25,689	6,661
Virginia	603	81	6,888	1,850	154,992	39,913
Washington	686	56	8,918	1,333	314,680	69,667
West Virginia	129	31	3,205	1,345	83,475	37,348
Wisconsin	424	73	4,367	1,129	188,626	54,452
Wyoming	82	13	894	223	54,472	19,022

Table D-4. Parameters a and b for Calculating Approximate Standard Errors of Sportspersons, Anglers, Hunters, and Wildlife-Watching Participants

(These parameters are to be used only to calculate estimates of standard errors for characteristics developed from the screening sample)

State	6 years old and older		6- to 15-year-olds only	
	a	b	a	b
United States............................	−0.000015	4,173	−0.000365	14,798
Alabama..........................	−0.000523	2,173	−0.014402	8,642
Alaska...........................	−0.001157	697	−0.024644	2,566
Arizona..........................	−0.000399	2,178	−0.008468	7,441
Arkansas.........................	−0.001116	2,820	−0.026111	9,698
California........................	−0.000126	4,134	−0.003139	16,914
Colorado.........................	−0.000573	2,435	−0.019382	12,522
Connecticut.......................	−0.000313	1,005	−0.008787	4,151
Delaware.........................	−0.000510	396	−0.014882	1,597
Florida	−0.000266	4,389	−0.006122	13,852
Georgia..........................	−0.000568	4,653	−0.012587	16,121
Hawaii	−0.000437	517	−0.009528	1,602
Idaho............................	−0.001346	1,759	−0.042091	8,654
Illinois...........................	−0.000296	3,416	−0.007029	12,542
Indiana	−0.000488	2,782	−0.012165	10,911
Iowa	−0.000762	2,062	−0.020347	7,491
Kansas	−0.000537	1,329	−0.016690	6,138
Kentucky	−0.000772	2,935	−0.018308	9,902
Louisiana	−0.000775	3,143	−0.017795	11,036
Maine	−0.000924	1,135	−0.030300	4,683
Maryland	−0.000357	1,821	−0.008162	6,298
Massachusetts.....................	−0.000261	1,521	−0.007130	5,692
Michigan.........................	−0.000685	6,318	−0.018937	26,784
Minnesota........................	−0.001009	4,733	−0.029835	20,037
Mississippi	−0.000757	1,982	−0.016992	6,865
Missouri	−0.000670	3,534	−0.018329	13,847
Montana	−0.001418	1,227	−0.033110	3,719
Nebraska.........................	−0.000567	902	−0.014086	3,277
Nevada	−0.000515	1,159	−0.011577	4,097
New Hampshire	−0.000535	650	−0.015945	2,744
New Jersey.......................	−0.000209	1,655	−0.005070	6,099
New Mexico.......................	−0.000620	1,097	−0.016872	4,557
New York.........................	−0.000320	5,582	−0.009275	22,967
North Carolina	−0.000416	3,286	−0.011916	14,068
North Dakota	−0.001096	637	−0.036240	2,677
Ohio.............................	−0.000484	5,045	−0.011219	17,172
Oklahoma	−0.000744	2,389	−0.020948	9,767
Oregon	−0.000752	2,533	−0.024824	11,839
Pennsylvania......................	−0.000544	6,176	−0.014615	22,903
Rhode Island	−0.000315	308	−0.008710	1,182
South Carolina	−0.000560	2,174	−0.016004	9,034
South Dakota	−0.001061	745	−0.025331	2,568
Tennessee	−0.000565	3,084	−0.015267	11,667
Texas............................	−0.000466	9,557	−0.011141	38,300
Utah	−0.000700	1,541	−0.018090	7,116
Vermont	−0.001053	611	−0.032724	2,420
Virginia..........................	−0.000450	3,102	−0.014313	14,311
Washington.......................	−0.000349	2,031	−0.010251	8,539
West Virginia	−0.001092	1,823	−0.042234	8,929
Wisconsin.........................	−0.000820	4,156	−0.021060	15,086
Wyoming	−0.001268	592	−0.028116	1,742

Table D-5. Parameters a and b for Calculating Approximate Standard Errors of Levels for the Detailed Sportspersons Sample

State	Sportspersons and anglers 16 years old and older		Hunters 16 years old and older	
	a	b	a	b
United States...........................	−0.000027	6,125	−0.000025	5,756
Alabama.......................	−0.000936	3,324	−0.000921	3,268
Alaska........................	−0.002197	1,096	−0.002013	1,004
Arizona.......................	−0.000641	2,941	−0.000403	1,849
Arkansas......................	−0.001833	3,951	−0.001705	3,674
California	−0.000239	6,523	−0.000213	5,801
Colorado......................	−0.000960	3,459	−0.000735	2,650
Connecticut...................	−0.000545	1,490	−0.000514	1,407
Delaware......................	−0.000758	507	−0.000720	482
Florida	−0.000415	5,911	−0.000347	4,943
Georgia.......................	−0.000965	6,668	−0.000752	5,199
Hawaii	−0.000763	774	−0.000751	761
Idaho.........................	−0.002486	2,738	−0.001888	2,080
Illinois.......................	−0.000430	4,201	−0.000388	3,789
Indiana	−0.000821	3,939	−0.000777	3,729
Iowa	−0.001383	3,234	−0.001535	3,589
Kansas	−0.001097	2,315	−0.001433	3,024
Kentucky	−0.001222	3,983	−0.001048	3,415
Louisiana	−0.001300	4,464	−0.001271	4,365
Maine	−0.001560	1,675	−0.001469	1,578
Maryland	−0.000552	2,392	−0.000456	1,975
Massachusetts.................	−0.000412	2,072	−0.000383	1,929
Michigan......................	−0.001085	8,470	−0.001214	9,474
Minnesota....................	−0.001694	6,812	−0.001504	6,049
Mississippi	−0.001355	3,000	−0.001169	2,588
Missouri......................	−0.001031	4,662	−0.001067	4,825
Montana	−0.002523	1,899	−0.002383	1,793
Nebraska......................	−0.001066	1,449	−0.001236	1,680
Nevada	−0.000898	1,703	−0.000823	1,561
New Hampshire	−0.000801	836	−0.000774	808
New Jersey....................	−0.000327	2,200	−0.000251	1,690
New Mexico...................	−0.001323	1,984	−0.001264	1,895
New York	−0.000456	6,842	−0.000378	5,671
North Carolina	−0.000713	4,794	−0.000588	3,951
North Dakota	−0.001558	791	−0.001754	890
Ohio	−0.000851	7,569	−0.000697	6,194
Oklahoma.....................	−0.001278	3,504	−0.001303	3,574
Oregon	−0.001291	3,730	−0.001024	2,957
Pennsylvania..................	−0.000867	8,490	−0.001030	10,089
Rhode Island	−0.000487	410	−0.000425	358
South Carolina	−0.000983	3,259	−0.000981	3,251
South Dakota	−0.001728	1,038	−0.001532	920
Tennessee	−0.001019	4,790	−0.000929	4,367
Texas.........................	−0.000859	14,660	−0.000725	12,388
Utah	−0.001453	2,627	−0.001268	2,292
Vermont	−0.001514	766	−0.001403	710
Virginia.......................	−0.000885	5,215	−0.001105	6,510
Washington....................	−0.000626	3,116	−0.000676	3,368
West Virginia	−0.001844	2,688	−0.001712	2,496
Wisconsin.....................	−0.001281	5,572	−0.001144	4,978
Wyoming	−0.003226	1,306	−0.002251	911

Table D-6. Parameters a, b, and c for Calculating Approximate Standard Errors for Expenditures for the Detailed Sportspersons Sample

State	Sportspersons and anglers 16 years old and older			Hunters 16 years old and older		
	a	b	c	a	b	c
United States.............................	**0.000118**	**–150,479**	**22,234**	**0.000918**	**–401,912**	**17,005**
Alabama	0.019700	–12,417	5,855	0.016799	–96,800	6,317
Alaska....................................	0.030420	–2,004	1,057	0.031018	–14,867	1,091
Arizona..................................	0.036222	–2,002	2,994	0.069395	–74,101	2,742
Arkansas.................................	0.024408	–27,794	6,433	0.010107	–101,205	7,942
California	0.018462	–35,800	10,686	0.027550	–58,262	9,255
Colorado.................................	0.008867	676	5,062	0.034102	–27,935	4,373
Connecticut..............................	0.036498	–11,421	2,841	0.096937	–60,991	2,564
Delaware.................................	0.031385	–1,643	734	0.018489	–3,855	719
Florida	0.014951	–23,048	9,553	0.021932	–407,268	10,425
Georgia	0.022339	–47,820	8,031	0.051440	–143,590	7,061
Hawaii	0.065152	–5,771	830	0.123487	–5,097	588
Idaho.....................................	0.034640	9,981	3,224	0.023728	–69,369	3,841
Illinois...................................	0.017187	6,704	5,219	0.024778	74,958	3,321
Indiana	0.027022	–16,160	4,558	0.042674	–61,618	4,557
Iowa	0.033205	22,341	2,171	0.045665	–41,343	1,583
Kansas	0.034206	–23,245	3,454	0.042600	–116,049	4,343
Kentucky	0.051496	–17,125	5,942	0.025277	–89,098	6,822
Louisiana	0.023308	–66,118	7,237	0.027891	135,631	6,412
Maine	0.022050	–7,457	2,175	0.021630	–12,360	2,038
Maryland	0.015599	–14,663	3,208	0.018873	–30,982	2,820
Massachusetts............................	0.049013	–25,362	3,792	0.138120	–47,649	2,049
Michigan.................................	0.035078	–148,672	13,535	0.039658	–147,585	12,587
Minnesota................................	0.028185	–92,976	11,279	0.027553	–263,285	12,919
Mississippi	0.026713	–53,218	5,433	0.014058	–97,282	6,390
Missouri	0.011821	–40,950	10,804	–0.005607	–190,726	17,070
Montana	0.024760	–9,845	2,520	0.020119	–99,543	3,580
Nebraska.................................	0.018618	1,031	1,640	0.022265	–22,187	1,472
Nevada	0.048609	–9,688	1,387	0.102222	–32,513	1,074
New Hampshire	0.025253	–6,176	1,434	0.037780	–26,900	1,448
New Jersey...............................	0.019672	–39,093	4,262	0.029909	–90,209	3,910
New Mexico..............................	0.084483	2,232	1,181	0.096226	20,132	683
New York	0.039569	–84,193	13,133	0.069695	–128,553	12,761
North Carolina	0.029775	–35,783	6,154	0.035333	–15,128	5,717
North Dakota	0.033611	–586	751	0.032562	6,176	804
Ohio	0.031480	–41,813	11,082	0.040646	–140,259	8,710
Oklahoma................................	0.023920	–27,206	4,719	0.020041	–31,920	5,066
Oregon	0.029208	–11,360	5,033	0.019440	–76,401	4,937
Pennsylvania.............................	0.011981	–92,207	15,295	0.014951	–17,951	14,434
Rhode Island	0.033545	–2,922	634	0.053976	–12,463	565
South Carolina	0.082716	–96,641	6,922	0.191600	–23,834	2,573
South Dakota	0.030933	682	1,071	0.018421	–25,518	1,356
Tennessee	0.027200	67,423	6,450	0.029272	–98,688	7,535
Texas.....................................	0.032817	–69,604	20,795	0.027826	–146,956	22,831
Utah......................................	0.033896	–13,369	2,671	0.024396	–195,230	4,439
Vermont	0.022379	–4,177	1,337	0.026395	–21,534	1,476
Virginia..................................	0.035897	–28,532	5,705	0.032298	–68,680	6,293
Washington...............................	0.026464	–45,106	5,612	0.081551	81,860	1,611
West Virginia	0.086611	–39,384	2,945	0.103915	–184,675	4,610
Wisconsin................................	0.017762	–81,329	10,849	0.029543	–54,069	8,015
Wyoming	0.075474	–5,404	1,197	0.090886	12,235	847

Table D-7. Parameters a, b, and c for Calculating Approximate Standard Errors for Days or Trips for the Detailed Sportspersons Sample

State	Sportspersons and anglers 16 years old and older			Hunters 16 years old and older		
	a	b	c	a	b	c
United States..........................	**0.000211**	**−23,610**	**23,157**	**−0.000235**	**−85,241**	**22,698**
Alabama	0.027360	−4,011	4,995	0.035544	−6,621	5,383
Alaska.	0.016117	−432	1,681	0.027498	8	1,622
Arizona.	0.065842	−511	1,775	0.053516	−8,367	2,773
Arkansas	0.013952	−12,325	8,675	0.024038	−5,931	6,861
California	0.010707	−16,022	13,917	0.028439	−23,877	12,350
Colorado.	0.019267	4,638	3,198	0.017940	128	3,608
Connecticut.	0.034363	−781	1,504	0.024306	−1,047	1,829
Delaware.	0.061308	−234	527	0.058226	−184	529
Florida	0.010264	−17,862	11,170	0.022310	21,695	5,794
Georgia.	0.040208	−10,805	6,234	0.044845	16,702	1,853
Hawaii	0.034563	−1,603	1,552	0.212584	−1,169	945
Idaho.	0.069064	−15,482	4,996	0.024568	−5,756	3,301
Illinois.	0.005932	−8,487	9,365	0.001562	−38,372	13,100
Indiana	0.006553	−5,775	6,973	0.018011	−6,028	6,053
Iowa	0.026962	−7,704	4,252	0.037766	−10,398	4,032
Kansas	0.015744	−2,510	4,078	0.046706	−21,946	6,195
Kentucky	0.015099	−6,026	7,313	−0.014871	−7,130	8,307
Louisiana	0.004012	−4,767	6,568	0.022152	−3,240	5,213
Maine	0.030520	−7,661	3,270	0.003096	−10,278	3,842
Maryland	0.017639	−6,240	3,697	0.011515	−6,512	3,608
Massachusetts.	0.027491	−3,619	4,355	0.044116	−8,700	5,301
Michigan.	0.011920	−23,905	20,643	0.025076	23,642	7,030
Minnesota	0.035500	−7,447	10,504	0.027723	−23,061	14,333
Mississippi	0.015625	−10,362	5,357	−0.000218	−2,695	4,394
Missouri	0.019454	−11,342	12,042	0.010034	−70,146	19,451
Montana	0.018290	−1,849	2,202	0.013948	−3,887	2,640
Nebraska.	0.009103	−2,063	3,655	−0.005553	−28,329	7,091
Nevada	0.043203	−1,733	1,536	0.123560	535	425
New Hampshire	0.019444	−2,643	1,627	0.013722	400	1,313
New Jersey.	0.026108	1,903	1,969	0.013215	−1,967	2,735
New Mexico.	0.112638	−431	817	0.096905	807	610
New York	0.029022	−22,367	14,881	0.008095	−27,096	17,017
North Carolina	0.021276	−6,354	5,499	0.012831	−28,563	9,265
North Dakota	0.019007	−3,002	1,621	0.008541	−5,760	2,617
Ohio.	0.022273	−21,768	15,604	0.044683	−9,949	10,955
Oklahoma.	0.006405	−10,237	8,296	0.013165	−12,426	8,445
Oregon	0.073495	−1,650	3,786	0.042692	−10,309	6,182
Pennsylvania.	0.027085	−24,417	16,685	−0.014656	−134,270	41,466
Rhode Island	0.011732	−506	680	0.021282	−344	525
South Carolina	0.014487	−6,537	6,823	0.086503	1,677	2,737
South Dakota	0.012863	−1,152	1,751	0.019075	−2,901	1,859
Tennessee	0.005611	−9,561	11,404	−0.011681	−60,797	16,711
Texas.	0.014288	−13,795	18,462	−0.003611	−31,876	25,228
Utah	0.041500	−1,853	2,544	0.071790	3,964	792
Vermont	0.016042	−1,485	1,360	−0.006963	−2,952	1,792
Virginia.	0.008112	−5,920	7,627	0.011922	165	6,590
Washington.	0.017168	−6,558	4,800	0.045009	3,663	1,723
West Virginia	0.006512	−2,872	4,433	0.001964	−2,897	4,911
Wisconsin	0.009197	−14,330	10,587	−0.002285	−35,565	15,098
Wyoming	0.025766	−1,835	1,823	0.034258	−3,738	1,705

Table D-8. Parameters a and b for Calculating Approximate Standard Errors of Levels of Wildlife-Watching Participants for the Detailed Wildlife-Watching Sample

State	Away-from-home participants		Wildlife-watching participants[1]	
	a	b	a	b
United States..	−0.000064	14,628	−0.000058	13,319
Alabama	−0.002522	8,955	−0.002252	7,994
Alaska...............................	−0.005091	2,539	−0.005744	2,864
Arizona..............................	−0.001212	5,555	−0.001128	5,170
Arkansas.............................	−0.003685	7,943	−0.003787	8,163
California	−0.000633	17,272	−0.000632	17,247
Colorado	−0.002818	10,157	−0.002773	9,995
Connecticut..........................	−0.001942	5,313	−0.001578	4,317
Delaware.............................	−0.002431	1,625	−0.002061	1,378
Florida	−0.001067	15,191	−0.001082	15,396
Georgia..............................	−0.002273	15,705	−0.002082	14,383
Hawaii	−0.002169	2,200	−0.002077	2,106
Idaho................................	−0.005872	6,469	−0.006027	6,640
Illinois..............................	−0.001350	13,189	−0.001237	12,083
Indiana..............................	−0.002090	10,031	−0.002026	9,722
Iowa	−0.003442	8,051	−0.003725	8,712
Kansas	−0.002087	4,403	−0.002245	4,737
Kentucky	−0.003921	12,780	−0.003130	10,201
Louisiana	−0.002878	9,878	−0.002325	7,980
Maine	−0.005383	5,779	−0.005003	5,372
Maryland	−0.001401	6,072	−0.001512	6,552
Massachusetts........................	−0.001153	5,803	−0.001045	5,260
Michigan.............................	−0.003188	24,879	−0.002805	21,892
Minnesota............................	−0.004869	19,579	−0.004257	17,116
Mississippi...........................	−0.004033	8,929	−0.004149	9,184
Missouri	−0.003241	14,653	−0.002731	12,349
Montana	−0.006536	4,919	−0.005006	3,768
Nebraska.............................	−0.001913	2,600	−0.001770	2,406
Nevada	−0.003763	7,131	−0.002387	4,524
New Hampshire	−0.002265	2,364	−0.002070	2,160
New Jersey...........................	−0.000942	6,346	−0.000899	6,057
New Mexico..........................	−0.002139	3,207	−0.002023	3,034
New York............................	−0.001498	22,454	−0.001320	19,791
North Carolina	−0.001307	8,785	−0.001368	9,194
North Dakota	−0.004745	2,408	−0.004900	2,486
Ohio	−0.001834	16,302	−0.001729	15,365
Oklahoma............................	−0.004720	12,946	−0.003724	10,214
Oregon	−0.004482	12,948	−0.003771	10,895
Pennsylvania.........................	−0.001862	18,235	−0.001779	17,426
Rhode Island	−0.001588	1,338	−0.001451	1,222
South Carolina	−0.002527	8,378	−0.002147	7,118
South Dakota	−0.005879	3,532	−0.005273	3,168
Tennessee............................	−0.002040	9,583	−0.002340	10,996
Texas................................	−0.002981	50,906	−0.002276	38,865
Utah	−0.002948	5,329	−0.003322	6,007
Vermont	−0.003834	1,940	−0.003687	1,866
Virginia..............................	−0.002142	12,625	−0.002049	12,078
Washington...........................	−0.001012	5,037	−0.001076	5,361
West Virginia	−0.005125	7,470	−0.005457	7,954
Wisconsin............................	−0.002461	10,707	−0.003232	14,058
Wyoming	−0.006998	2,833	−0.006562	2,657

[1] Use these parameters for total wildlife-watching participants and around-the-home participants.

Table D-9. Parameters a, b, and c for Calculating Approximate Standard Errors for Expenditures and Days or Trips for Wildlife-Watching Participants

State	Expenditures			Days or trips		
	a	b	c	a	b	c
United States............................	**0.000184**	**–1,140,662**	**67,137**	**0.000574**	**1,457,630**	**–8,497**
Alabama................................	0.045588	–11,994	16,603	0.188740	–119,343	614
Alaska..................................	0.120206	–27,366	3,041	–0.124071	–135,739	22,893
Arizona.................................	0.030207	–53,304	10,729	–0.012992	48,146	15,350
Arkansas...............................	0.099812	14,720	8,751	–0.017705	122,002	28,315
California	0.033850	–512,106	41,075	–0.045068	409,984	182,262
Colorado................................	0.027999	–274,128	22,499	–0.048837	–38,813	65,367
Connecticut.............................	0.021634	–65,691	10,399	–0.024457	–95,765	25,345
Delaware...............................	0.065106	–1,447	1,138	–0.008505	9,777	5,498
Florida	0.023886	346,119	21,198	0.008852	367,813	29,038
Georgia.................................	0.074762	–1,010,585	34,617	–0.043108	–269,579	83,544
Hawaii	0.083826	–21,578	2,574	–0.072050	–22,450	10,110
Idaho...................................	0.062974	–42,113	7,740	–0.034736	–28,632	22,517
Illinois..................................	0.036256	–247,805	22,614	–0.015710	–127,759	55,397
Indiana.................................	0.036663	–31,127	16,250	–0.011371	–60,979	38,357
Iowa	0.079272	54,459	5,841	–0.010582	–64,612	23,312
Kansas	0.065343	2,002	6,423	–0.009647	290,376	9,046
Kentucky	0.054215	7,733	10,118	–0.027046	–203,563	66,052
Louisiana	0.122208	–20,968	9,262	–0.027645	11,297	25,905
Maine	0.023874	–51,089	9,384	–0.124695	–361,658	61,734
Maryland	0.014472	–4,594	10,674	0.003905	125,364	13,230
Massachusetts...........................	0.028723	–178,823	9,836	–0.028071	–151,233	43,446
Michigan................................	0.034044	–350,268	38,895	–0.189982	–1,478,372	355,858
Minnesota..............................	0.074185	–156,337	26,053	–0.037135	–287,075	81,476
Mississippi..............................	0.069734	–5,671	8,343	0.007734	–4,828	12,669
Missouri................................	0.050350	–370,879	19,939	–0.072363	–297,324	107,372
Montana................................	0.096467	–101,441	7,127	0.021739	75,970	2,590
Nebraska................................	0.057553	–29,126	3,150	–0.037603	–53,492	15,634
Nevada.................................	0.114708	–32,736	5,704	0.007035	8,360	8,647
New Hampshire	0.014724	–17,918	4,039	–0.004938	74,043	4,376
New Jersey	0.022949	–169,333	13,969	–0.040442	238,149	40,992
New Mexico.............................	0.036652	16,768	4,306	–0.023441	72,449	11,803
New York...............................	0.042036	–450,788	32,575	–0.019285	–366,511	102,534
North Carolina..........................	0.061423	–16,794	13,694	–0.012815	19,657	37,216
North Dakota...........................	0.155007	–2,199	1,794	0.150664	6,024	376
Ohio	0.035458	–205,570	28,049	–0.018753	–103,758	63,267
Oklahoma...............................	0.036357	–21,977	15,171	–0.000564	1,344,926	16,961
Oregon	0.062814	–65,011	9,965	–0.004734	831,881	37,513
Pennsylvania............................	0.054585	–176,791	24,331	–0.024636	–296,844	94,825
Rhode Island	0.037242	–31	2,537	–0.019391	234	7,490
South Carolina	0.017341	–52,304	14,141	–0.021836	–45,588	28,960
South Dakota	0.058011	–16,346	3,878	–0.063876	–12,873	14,245
Tennessee	0.058962	–19,581	19,197	–0.067979	539,487	98,190
Texas...................................	0.107126	268,978	41,639	–0.115263	–2,660,430	425,213
Utah	0.056246	–5,750	4,842	–0.002938	–77,345	25,347
Vermont	0.005556	–22,018	4,065	–0.014449	33,588	6,073
Virginia.................................	0.043764	–51,970	12,817	–0.046070	–227,508	91,189
Washington.............................	0.030615	–16,210	11,199	–0.000250	36,174	12,719
West Virginia	0.118586	–4,653	8,819	–0.073404	38,459	30,640
Wisconsin...............................	0.009997	–400,732	26,411	–0.015178	–125,383	46,927
Wyoming	0.083907	–31,350	3,012	–0.062286	–29,913	12,976

Notes

www.ingramcontent.com/pod-product-compliance
Lightning Source LLC
Chambersburg PA
CBHW052005280526
45793CB00005B/859